MEMOIR ON THE ISLAND OF SOCOTRA

JAMES WELLSTED

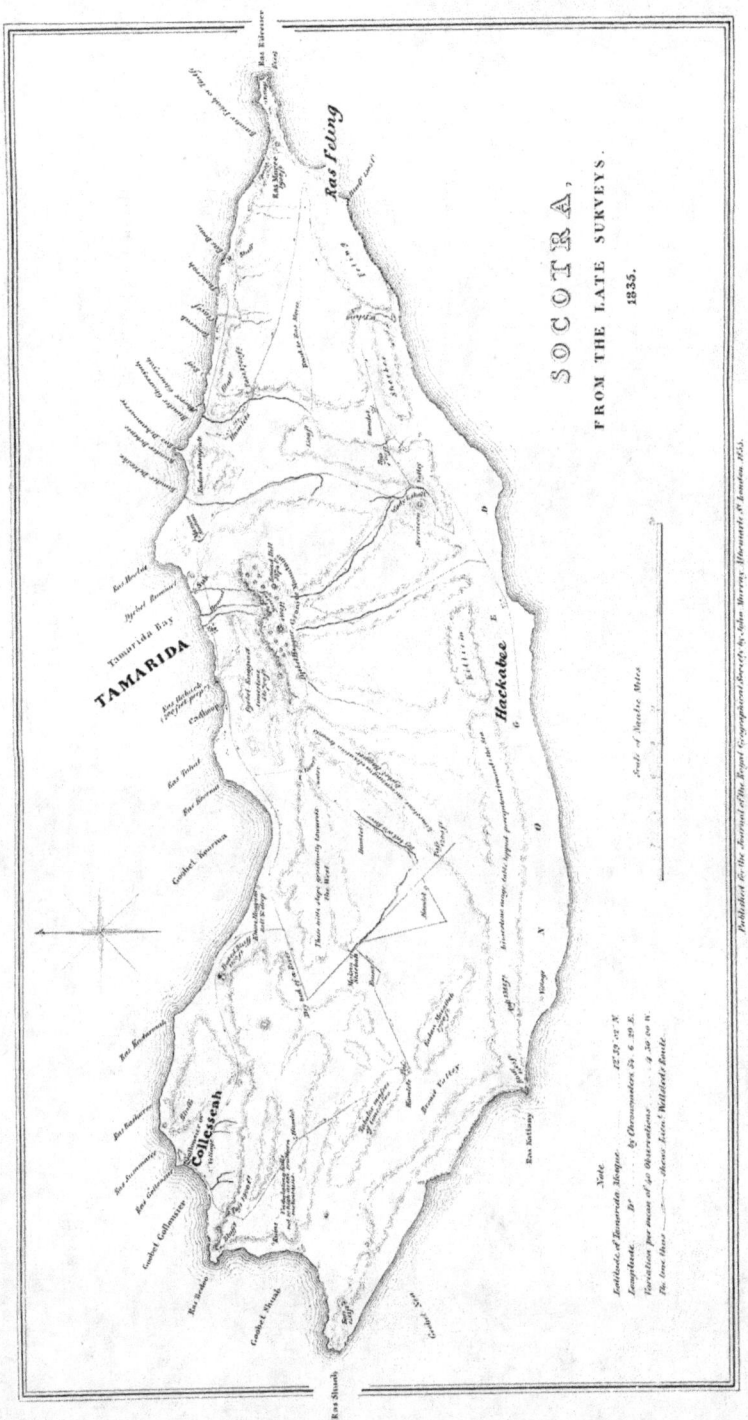

CONTENTS

INTRODUCTION THIS EDITION — vii

1. Hadibu — 1
2. Departure For Qalansiyah — 10
3. Finding Dragon's Blood Trees — 34
4. Return To Hadibu — 49
5. Departure To Hackabee & Southern Coast — 53
6. Travel To Ras Feling — 62
7. Return To Palinurus — 68
8. Background To Socotra — 73
9. Language — 96

Notations — 107
index — 109
Photographs — 115

INTRODUCTION THIS EDITION

This edition of *Memoir on the Island of Socotra* has been retyped, keeping to James Wellsted's original, but sometimes varying, style, grammar and spelling. The exceptions are in the names of structures, places and individuals where in his text there were different spellings within the book. This is so that there can be no doubt that they are one and the same. There are some names where certainty is impossible. Wellstead wrote about the "*eshaib*" tree. In some instances he appears to describe the Dragons Blood Tree (*Dracaena cinnabari*) with a "natural bower formed by the umbrageous foliage", in others possibly Socotra Fig (*Ficus socotrana*) "in its light and graceful form, the weeping-ash of England". So with this uncertainty – in all cases the *eshaib* is retained. Place names have also been revised so that the modern name is used. Therefore Hadibu (Tamarida), Qishn (Kisseen) and so on. This is so that not only is there consistency in spelling, but modern mapping can also be referred to – the original spelling is bracketed in the first instance. The inclusion of ordinals after dates was inconsistent, and February 13 was included twice in his dating, or did the typesetters make a mistake on the first for 12? Though the original book's type was modern English, the map used the older style long 's' as in paſs, for pass.

The original text had no need for chapters; it was presented as a talk. In this edition the chapters are therefore entirely introduced, to aid navigation.

Supporting modern images have been included.

The book is initially in the form of a dated diary, offering detailed insights into the people he met on his journey, together with their culture. The later chapters offer a wider perspective of Socotra.

JAMES RAYMOND WELLSTED

James Raymond Wellsted was born in 1805. His father, also named James Wellsted, worked as an upholsterer. James Wellsted senior may have been among the first tenants of Molyneux Street, Marylebone – part of the Portman Estate of north-central London, developed for the Portman family, descendants of Sir William Portman, a Tudor magnate and royal servant.

Little is known of our James Wellsted's early life. His sister, Sophia Matilda Wellsted – later the wife of solicitor J. D. Marsden – was the mother of Kate Marsden, the explorer and Christian missionary. Kate somehow secured a personal audience in 1890 with Queen Victoria and, later that same year, with Princess Alexandra, the future Queen – and, even more improbably, with the Empress of Russia, who thirteen years earlier had honoured her for humanitarian work with wounded soldiers in Bulgaria. James Wellsted had an earlier close encounter with Queen Victoria; the family possessed either remarkable chutzpah or an extraordinary "six degrees of separation."

James Raymond Wellsted entered the East India Company's (EIC) naval service, the Bombay Marine, in 1823 as a Volunteer; the cadet grade from which officers advanced. The term dated from the eighteenth century and denoted young men offering service without a formal commission: "volunteers" not in the modern sense of unpaid helpers, but in contrast to those "press-ganged" into service. His first ship was HCS *Ternate*, a 237-ton, 18-gun brig launched in 1801. Though used as a survey vessel, the *Ternate* had taken part in the British attack on Ras Al Khaimah in 1819.

Wellsted's next few years were spent in the Persian Gulf, on what was a multi-purpose assignment. The Bombay Marine brig/sloop *Ternate* was primarily a survey vessel, though it was also used for armed attacks and for diplomatic dispatches. With perhaps 150 men and no more than 20 officers, it wasn't a large ship. From 1827, Wellsted gives a snapshot of its work – and of himself.

"While cruising on this coast in 1827, I was proceeding with dispatches to the Sheikh of Sharjah, Sultan bin Saqr, when a strong breeze unexpectedly set in...our boat...was capsized... After landing, the gale increased, and for three days we could not attempt to put off to the vessel (the *Ternate*)... Sultan was unremitting in his attention to me... On one occasion he invited me to dine... a small room... a rude table, two or three chairs, given him by the commanders of our vessels... [and] coffee, which the Sheikh himself made and handed round. A storyteller was then called in... but I was then too ignorant of the language to understand it."

This small episode reveals the traits that made Wellsted a perceptive traveller: calm in a capsize, curious in a majlis, and courteous enough to take the carpet over the gifted chairs. Wellsted understood his environment and was eager to fit in.

Wellsted was one of a compact cohort of contemporaries – junior officers who would criss-cross the Indian Ocean and the Persian Gulf. Henry Lynch joined the

Ternate on the same day as Wellsted; Henry Ormsby joined 7 June 1823 and served in the 387-ton *Elphinstone*; and Edward Wyburd, who became 2nd Lieutenant in the 420-ton *Amherst* on 9 July 1825. These men were part of what was a surprisingly small number of officers in the Bombay Marine (Indian Navy). In 1830 there were probably fewer than 160, all European, from the Superintendent (Sir Charles Malcolm) down to the Midshipmen. Indian sailors crewed the ships. The total crew number on the 18 ships of the Bombay Marine was between 2,100 and 2,700.

In *City of the Caliphs*, Wellsted reflected on his contemporaries' restless range: "It is a singular fact that so small a service as the Indian Navy should, in one and the same year, have seven midshipmen, four of whom have traversed more of the East than probably the same number of individuals alive; Ormsby, Lynch, W[yburd], and, may I add, the editor of these volumes." Their choice of the EIC's service (the Bombay Marine until 1830, when it was retitled the Indian Navy) was likely helped by the Royal Navy's post-Napoleonic contraction: many British naval ships were laid up, and opportunities afloat narrowed.

Sir Henry Creswicke Rawlinson, writing in 1873, placed Lynch "of the school of Ormsby, Wellsted, and Wyburd" – an accurate and daring observer, and, he thought, the most gifted of the group as a scholar and linguist.

The East India Company's strategic outlook had shifted after the Napoleonic Wars. In 1799 the defeat of Tipu Sultan, whose father had seized the throne of Mysore, removed a principal adversary within India; Napoleon's failure in Egypt and the French evacuation in 1801 blunted the immediate French threat to India. Although Napoleon later sent Jean-Baptiste de Cavaignac to Muscat in 1803 to try and gain wide-scale support, he returned empty-handed. After Waterloo, British command of the sea from London to Bombay was unchallenged, and within India the EIC held sway. Yet in *Travels in Arabia* Wellsted warned that the French spectre had given way to anxiety over Russia's southward reach: he wrote "The Russian frontier now extends to within 120 miles of the sources of the Euphrates... the passage of an army along its banks to the shores of the Persian Gulf might be accomplished without any considerable difficulty." From Bombay's vantage point, the Great Game was beginning.

Steam power changed the tempo at sea. After early coastal experiments, and with deep-sea passages proven from the 1810s onward, Bombay's Government grew keen to employ steam for its own long-distance routes. The arrival from London, in 1825, of the auxiliary paddle steamer *Enterprise*, into Calcutta, showed what might now be possible between London and Bombay via the Cape, though it turned out that the Red Sea would become critical.

The Malcolms – Sir John Malcolm, appointed Governor of Bombay on 1 November 1827, and his brother Captain Sir Charles Malcolm, brought in as Superintendent of the Marine – pressed for "full steam ahead" in policy and propulsion. Charles Malcolm, a 45-year-old Royal Navy officer, seasoned in the

Indian Ocean, the West Indies, South America, and the Atlantic, reached Bombay on 1 June 1828 and took up his post on Wednesday, 4 June. The young Wellsted served as his secretary.

Steam power to serve India had powerful champions with the Malcolm brothers and their brother Sir Pulteney Malcolm, naval Commander-in-Chief in the Mediterranean. The 411-ton paddle-steamer HCS *Hugh Lindsay* was launched at Bombay on 14 October 1829 in the Malcolms' presence (and, one suspects, that of the Superintendent's secretary).

In 1829 the survey sloop HCS *Thetis* escorted a single collier up the Red Sea, depositing hard Welsh "steam coal" that burned hot, with low ash and little smoke, at Aden, Jeddah, Quseir and Suez; the collier was wrecked on the return – an object lesson in why Moresby's charts, completed soon after, were not a luxury but a necessity. The coal was to allow the *Hugh Lindsay* to make its maiden voyage from Bombay.

From Bombay, *Hugh Lindsay* made its proving voyage in March 1830 to Suez. With almost all spare space in the ship given over to coal, her twin 80-horsepower engines burned roughly seventeen tons a day. The round voyage – Bombay–Suez–Bombay – took forty-one days door-to-door. Underway, she averaged about six knots (11 km/h); the coaling halts pulled the overall average down. Modern expedition-type small cruise ships run at around 15 knots, so *Hugh Lindsay* was no speedster. Even so, the verdict was clear to the Malcolms – and soon the EIC: steam was the future. *Hugh Lindsay* made regular mail runs up the Red Sea, for onward delivery to London and eventually worked in the Persian Gulf and Shatt al-Arab.

When *Hugh Lindsay* later cruised in the Persian Gulf, she drew both amazement and dismay. In waters long ruled by monsoon and shamal winds – where the wind direction can come from one direction for months, steam power promised year-round navigation to any point of the compass. However, the ship was only half the story: steam demanded coal depots and soundings – bunkering stations and hydrographic surveys – the essential foundations of naval supremacy.

In 1830, aged twenty-five, Wellsted was sent to chart the Arabian coasts aboard HCS (Honourable Company's Ship) *Palinurus* – aptly named for Aeneas's helmsman – as the classical Erythraean Sea was mapped so that modern steam could run through ancient waters.

From 1830 the EIC split the work between two small brigs: HCS *Palinurus* (8 guns; 192 tons bm ["builder's measurement"]) under Captain Robert Moresby for the northern Red Sea, and HCS *Benares* (14 guns; 230 tons bm) under Captain Thomas Elwon for the southern half.

James Raymond Wellsted joined *Palinurus* as second lieutenant in October 1830. On that service he noted the brig carried seventy men; twenty-five Europeans and forty-five lascar ratings – a distribution shaped by survey work with multiple cutters, shore parties, instrument-keepers, and draughtsmen.

A survey lieutenant's core duties were to fix latitude and longitude by observation (with chronometers rated to Greenwich), run systematic lines of soundings from the cutters or more often by negotiating with local boat owners, lead shore parties to establish points and sketch coastal profiles, and compile boat-sheets and fair copies. Wellsted also compiled details of the supplies available at ports. From these, Captain Moresby, with Lieut. T. G. Carless, produced the detailed sea charts that were refined in Bombay and usually sent to John Walker's office in London to be engraved as the finished Red Sea series. Wellsted's logs also fed the *Sailing Directions for the Red Sea* (issued with Horsburgh's *India Directory*, 5th ed., 1841), forming the new hydrography into practical routing.

Palinurus was a compact vessel – roughly the size of the 180-ton *Mayflower*. Her size and draught let her thread among coral reefs and sand bars, hazards that increased on the approaches to major ports such as Jeddah. As was usual in the early 19th century, copper sheathing would give protection against marine wood-borers, but minimal protection against grounding on coral reefs that were so common in the Red Sea.

Beyond the charts, Wellsted produced sailing directions, coastal views, and narratives that circulated within the Bombay Marine. Two centuries on, his descriptions of inland journeys still matter for understanding the EIC's forward planning, most notably his weeks on Socotra, then under active consideration for one or more coaling stations between Bombay and Suez. The portrait that emerges is of a confident – at times overconfident – but non-judgemental observer of the places he passed through.

Wellsted was explicit about the practical aim of the Red Sea work: "To ascertain how far its passage could be made available for steamers was one of the principal objects to which our attention was directed during the late survey of the Red Sea." He also wrote with a frank Anglo-centric confidence: "Egypt, the high-way between Europe and India, must, sooner or later, be ours. How gladly its present wretched inhabitants would hail the change, let those answer who have visited it, instead of drawing their ideas of the government of its enlightened ruler from reports current in Europe."

Like many nineteenth-century travelogues, his narrative of these surveys jump-cuts – sometimes zigzagging like a dhow beating into a headwind – so the sequence and even the spellings shift on the page. Thus Cosseir appears as Kosa'ir on the next page (I used Quseir as the most usual today); Terhan becomes Tiran. The *Palinurus* first sailed down the Arabian coast (modern Saudi Arabia) from Ras Muhammad at the Sinai tip, then went across to the Tiran narrows and south to Al Muwaylih with its fort. The fort, built around AD 1560, dates from soon after the Ottomans' control of the Hijaz. It was one of a string of forts built not only to control the region but also to provide support to Hajj pilgrims. The Hajj pilgrims travelled in vast caravans from Egypt and Syria that followed the coastline, while those from India and beyond would use one of the ports serving Madinah and Makkah.

On land, Muhammad Ali Pasha held Egypt to an extent from 1805, but indisputably from his massacre of the Mamluks in the Cairo Citadel in 1811; the Hijaz was an historical possession of whoever ruled Egypt. However, after the naval battle at Navarino (20 October 1827) and the Egyptian and Ottoman defeat, Britain enjoyed de facto maritime supremacy in the Red Sea as well as the Mediterranean. The increasing use of steam power needing physical coaling stations and the imminent charts would only increase that domination.

The *Palinurus* coasted south to Jeddah, in effect parallel to the Egyptian Hajj road; Wellsted put arriving sea-borne pilgrims from Egypt at around 20,000, and India had 2,000 arriving annually. Jeddah intrigued Wellsted for its people and its markets – "goods and food" in profusion – but his understandable focus was the dynamics and interplay of Muhammad Ali's officers, the Sherifs of Makkah and the recent exclusion of the Ottomans.

In 1832, the *Palinurus* shifted north to survey the Sinai, where Wellsted made excursions in biblically resonant terrain, where he wrote about Moses and Elim in the belief that southern Sinai was a location for both. With Lieutenant Thomas G. Carless (the draughtsman), he also travelled overland between Quseir and Luxor in Egypt.

Quseir – Luxor – Cairo – Alexandria offered one conceivable overland/river bridge between London and Bombay, but the Suez–Cairo–Alexandria route won out. The Red Sea survey work by *Palinurus* was completed between 1830 and 1833. The resulting charts – compiled by Moresby and Carless and published by John Walker – appeared in 1836.

Lieutenant Wellsted's next assignment was under Captain Stafford B. Haines, still in *Palinurus*. In October 1833, they set off for a survey of southern and eastern Arabia, starting from Ras Madrakah (then styled by British chart-makers as Cape Isoletta) in Eastern Oman. Moving south to Qishn in Mahrah in Yemen, Haines sought a formal agreement from the Mahrah tribe's Sultan Amar bin Saad bin Tawari to survey Socotra, which the Mahrah tribe ruled. From 9 January to 14 March 1834 the ship's boats traced the island's coasts; ashore, Wellsted, who was then Assistant-Surveyor, and Midshipman Charles Cruttenden crossed the interior.

Wellsted's *Memoir on the Island of Socotra* covers 10 January–7 March 1834. His party comprised Hamid who was the guide (though dismissed mid-journey for obstructiveness), Sulayman who ultimately proved to be the most useful guide, a Nubian boy named Sunday, an Indian cook, and two enslaved men from the island for general duties. Their start coincided with Ramadan 1249 AH (11 Jan–9/10 Feb 1834), which inevitably complicated how the journey was managed. Transport was by camel (*Camelus dromedarius*). Luggage was lashed high, and somehow "beds" were balanced onto the top of that luggage. Wellsted quips that it resulted in him perched fourteen feet above the ground; he must have swayed dramatically with the stride of the animal. At Hadibu (then Tamarida – the name is linked to *tamar*, the Arabic for the date palm *Phoenix dactylifera*), a local sheikh objected to the party's wanderings and Cruttenden stayed with him as a good-conduct hostage during the midpoint of the circuit. Even with the almost inevitable hindrances, the exploration achieved its essential aims.

The surveys triggered the Government of India to attempt to purchase Socotra as a coaling-station and authorised an offer of up to 10,000 Maria Theresa thalers (the regional trade coin originally from Austria) – but the Sultan refused outright. Nonetheless, a small mixed detachment (European and Indian) under Captain R. A. Bayly had already been sent and landed at Hadibu in late 1834. Disease soon ravaged their camp; contemporary accounts remarked that scarcely a sound man remained to dig his comrade's grave. The detachment was shifted up into the hills, then withdrawn in stages between April and November 1835. British interest in Socotra as a coal depot faded, and with Aden taken in 1839, Socotra regained its former obscurity, making Wellsted's account even more valuable.

Wellsted spent the rest of 1834 and much of 1835 surveying the southern coasts of Arabia between Ras Madrakah and Aden. Once again Cruttenden joined Wellsted on a several-day journey of exploration into a valley 370 km northeast of Aden. This turned out to have been a near disaster. "It was not indeed until afterwards that we ascertained the extreme risk we had encountered on this journey; for the Diyabi Bedouins, finding we had passed through their territory, lay in wait for us, under the impression we should return by the same route. But the ship fortunately took up a second station, about twenty miles to the westward of the former one, and on receiving intelligence of that, we returned by another and more direct road to her."

By mid-1835 Wellsted had left the *Palinurus* on the Aden–Mokha sector and returned to Bombay. There, he must have used his earlier service as Sir Charles Malcolm's secretary (1828–29), as he secured Bombay Government permission for an inland exploration of Oman – that he also hoped would enable him to visit the capital of what is now termed the Second Saudi State in Riyadh (he referred to it as their previous capital Diriyah).

Wellsted wrote, "After obtaining the necessary permission, I embarked at Bombay on board a small schooner (the *Cysene*) for Muscat, at which port, after a pleasant passage, we arrived on the 21st of November. I found Sayyid Said, the Imam of Muscat or sovereign of Oman, ready, with his characteristic liberality, in every way to forward my views. Letters were prepared under his own direction to the chiefs of the different districts through which I had to pass, and on November 25th I quitted that port to proceed to Sur."

Travelling, supported by a small party through Oman, often into areas known to be hostile to any traveller, Wellsted displayed an almost naive trust, which enabled him to undertake his journeys. This trust was his characteristic outlook, but it was tempered with some preparedness. In Yemen he "knew that the natives of this district were considered especially hostile to those of a different creed; and that they had some years ago cut off the whole of a boat's crew of the only vessel that had previously touched on their coast, by seducing them with promises from the beach, I could not, therefore, but accuse myself of rashness, in thus venturing with no better pledge for our safety than their promised fidelity." Though while in Socotra, he noted when an Arab "suggested, indeed, that any individual, seated, as he was, near me, could seize me by the wrist or throat, so as to render me powerless, while his companions might plunder the baggage; but a sight of the pistols, which I always wore concealed at my girdle, convinced him that I was anything but defenceless against open attacks."

Irrespective of the location, the inhabitants of most towns and villages he visited in Oman were reluctant to support the onward travel of Wellsted. This was either from their stated belief that the journey itself was dangerous or to show hospitality and keep him with them – in traditional Omani society, three days was considered an appropriate stay. Nonetheless, Wellsted usually overcame their arguments and continued with his travels.

Arriving in Bani bu Ali, Oman, the location of two intense battles between the eponymous Arab tribe and British forces fifteen years earlier, he received "a reception so truly warm and hospitable not a little surprised me. Before us lay the ruins of the fort we had dismantled, my tent was pitched on the very spot where we had nearly annihilated their tribe, reducing them from being the most powerful in Oman to their present petty state. All, however, in the confidence I had shown in thus throwing myself amidst them, was forgotten." Wellsted's confidence and presumably manner almost acted as a guarantor of his safety. He travelled alone, for several days, escorted by a party of Janaba Bedouin. They reached deep into the sand desert, enabling him to gain remarkable insight into their character and culture.

Wellsted was remarkably stoic; in Yemen, his guides abandoned him in a remote area. "Unexpectedly, however, we fell in with an old woman, who, as soon as she was informed of our situation, without the slightest hesitation promised to conduct us to her house. We gladly followed her, but having wandered far from the path, we did not arrive there until midnight. We found our guides comfortably seated within a house, smoking their pipes and drinking coffee. Though excessively provoked, I was aware that remonstrance would be useless; and concealing my chagrin, I proceeded to secure a lodging for the night."

He was a most observant and insightful traveller, remarking in Oman that "Although the Grand Sheikhs of the principal tribes have in some cases the power of life and death, and also that of declaring war and peace, yet their authority in every instance is considerably abridged by the aged and other influential men of the tribe. In civil and criminal affairs they act rather as arbiters than as judges, and cases of importance are sometimes debated by the whole tribe." This was the case in Oman until at least the mid-20th century, and in some instances of matters of social importance to a tribe, up to the current day.

Wellsted's courtesy, good manners and confidence in those he met were ideally suited to the society he met. "After their evening prayers, the young Sheikh, accompanied by about forty men, came to the tent, and expressed his intention of remaining with me as a guard during the night. To ask the whole party in was impossible, and to invite a few only would have displeased others, so I took my carpet outside amidst them."

Unlike Wilfred Thesiger who in the mid-20th century travelled far more extensively in Arabia, but perhaps deliberately avoided the company or mention of women, Wellsted mixed easily with females. In Oman, "The women were seated on an old carpet near a good fire, and I was invited to place myself between them. They were unveiled and entered freely into conversation with me. After answering a hundred questions connected with the English and their country, coffee, and then milk, were introduced."

Wellsted frequently expressed considerable admiration of the women he met, perhaps no more so than in Suwaiq recounting when the Sheikh's wife, a sister of Oman's ruler Sayyid Said, "heard the intelligence [of a planned attack by her brother Sayyid Said on the town during her husband's captivity, who was held by Sayyid Said in Muscat as hostage], she sent messengers to collect the various Bedouin tribes who were in the interest of her husband, and made other preparations to march in person against the dominions of the Imam; but before any succours could arrive, the latter had despatched a force to Suwaiq, in order to take possession of the fort, with an assurance, that unless it was given up, the Sheikh should be put to death. 'Go back' said this spirited female, when the message was delivered to her; 'Go back to those who sent you, and tell them that I will defend the fort to the utmost of my power; and if they choose to cut him to pieces before me, they will find it make no alteration in my resolution.' She accordingly defended it with so much bravery and skill, that the Imam's force, after losing several men and wasting considerable time, were compelled to raise the siege and proceed to Muscat."

Wellsted's attitude was not always one of admiration of all he met; "It will apply as a general re-mark, that the Sheikhs of the towns in Oman are very personable men, with a dignified deportment and pleasing manners; but this was a sneaking, greasy-looking animal, who had more the appearance of a butcher than a Sheikh."

Remarkably open to other cultures, Wellsted also accepted that individuals were not representative of a general population. In Yemen he explained; "Our guides, as usual, having gone to seek shelter from the heat of the sun, had left us to make our breakfast on dates and water, in any sheltered spot we could find. The sun was nearly vertical, and the walls of the houses afforded us no protection. Seeing this, several of the inhabitants came forward, and offered with much kindness to take us to their dwellings. We gladly consented and followed one of them. Coffee was immediately served; and it was with some difficulty, after a promise to return if possible in the evening, that we prevented our host from ordering a meal to be immediately cooked for us. This circumstance, combined with several others which occurred on our return, convinced me, if we had been provided with a better escort, that after passing the territory of the Diyabis, we should have experienced neither incivility nor unkindness from the people."

Wellsted had the account of the Socotra read to the Royal Geographical Society in London in 1835 and published his Red Sea/Southern Arabia travels in 1838 as Volume 2 of *Travels in Arabia*. This is an amalgam of several visits to the Red Sea region over six years. The narrative includes Pharaonic history, Biblical history, and recent events, all wrapped in descriptions of the areas in which Wellsted travelled. He notes details constantly; "Locusts are sold in the markets of Yanbu, and also at Jeddah. The Mukin or Red species, being the fattest, is preserved, and, when fried and sprinkled with salt, they are considered wholesome and nutritious food" – this practice has continued down to modern times. Continual references are made as to the relations of tribes with the Ottoman Turks and Egypt's Mohammed Ali, who were, at least nominally, the region's rulers.

Wellsted's publication of *Travels in Arabia* cemented his reputation as an author. Published in 1838, it was dedicated in December 1837, with her permission, to the new Queen, Victoria, quite an audience for the former naval "volunteer".

The press highly commended the publication. After expressing its "high admiration of the diligence and talent shown by Lieutenant Wellsted," one paper says, "the Memoir does credit both to the author himself and to the Service to which he belongs."

Wellsted, however, did not have good health on his journeys. In 1834, while travelling through Socotra, Wellsted and his party became ill with "fever", possibly malaria. Again, while in Oman in the winter 1835/6, Wellsted, along with all his party, collapsed with "fever", whose symptoms do suggest malignant (falciparum) malaria – requiring lengthy recuperation.

During the year following Wellsted's first exploration to Oman he continued working on the *Palinurus*. Once again the ship was surveying the coasts of southern Oman and Yemen, though given his published papers he must also have been writing on board. While surveying the Hallaniyat Islands, off the coast of Dhofar, the *Palinurus* rescued the crew of the whaling ship *Reliance*, which was hunting for whales, most likely sperm whales for their blubber. The Hallaniyat Islands seemed to be a magnet for ships destined to be wrecked; the most famous is probably the Portuguese vessel *Esmerelda* which sank in a storm in 1503.

Visiting Oman again in April 1837, he was again in an acute stage of "fever". A Victorian commentator wrote that; "In a fit of delirium he discharged both barrels of his gun into his mouth, but the balls, passing upwards, only inflicted two ghastly wounds in the upper jaw." He was transported from Oman aboard the *Hugh Lindsay* (that amazing steamship) to Bombay and thence returned to Europe on leave, reluctantly leaving his Arab horse behind.

Wellsted was a sought-after expert about the region, giving evidence to the House of Commons in 1837 about the Red Sea steamship route. He was retired from the Indian Navy on 9 May 1838 and, according to commentators, dragged on a few years in shattered health and with impaired mental powers, recuperating in France. Though despite that mention of Wellsted's health, he wrote extensively and fluently.

During this period he wrote *Travels to the City of Caliphs*, which was published in 1840. This book was compiled from Henry Ormsby's accounts to Wellsted of Ormsby's travels between 1826 and 1830 and a previous manuscript written by Ormsby. Wellsted, in effect, was acting as a mouthpiece for Ormsby. After his adventures, Ormsby re-entered the navy, he was, after all, one of those four acclaimed young men, so was a welcome returnee. Ormsby was rapidly rising up the ranks, even serving in the China war of 1840–1842 and must have been too busy to complete his memoir.

Wellsted, writing in the preface of *Travels to the City of Caliphs* "This work owes its origin to the following circumstance. Lieut. (Henry) Ormsby, of the Indian Navy, the hero of the first part of the work, voluntarily quitted that service at the early age of nineteen and devoted himself for three years to traversing various portions of the East. The buoyancy of spirit with which every hardship encountered by my friend was surmounted; his courage, and zealous perseverance, where others, amidst pestilence and famine, would have shrunk back, and the facility with which he filled up the variety of characters it was necessary he should assume, are perhaps unequalled even amidst the performances of the host of celebrated travellers to whom it has been the pride of Great Britain to have given birth. If the several incidents therefore are not portrayed with sufficient strength, the fault lies with the author and not the adventurer".

Wellsted was considerate of others, even during his first fever in Oman. Then, while he was recovering in Seeb, he paid for the sea transport from Muscat to Seeb and subsequent care costs for a Frenchman who was ill in Muscat.

On 25 October 1842, Wellsted died at 13 Molyneux Street, aged 37. His will named his father, James Wellsted, as the only beneficiary – of £100, a modest sum in those days.

Wellsted's reputation was maligned in subsequent memoirs and marginalia. Captain Haines wrote in the *Transactions of the Bombay Geographical Society*, published 1852–53, "the late Lieutenant Wellsted, of the Indian Navy, appears to have caused an erroneous account" (of Wellsted's role in Socotra). Haines describes the context "I decided, therefore, that, while I conducted the trigonometrical survey of the island, my assistant [he meant Wellsted] should travel leisurely through the interior; and, to assist him, I ordered Mr. Midshipman (now Lieutenant) Cruttenden, who understood the Arab language and character well, to accompany him. Having executed the commands of Government within the time specified, I forwarded a fair copy of my survey, with my own observations on its anchorages, and those of my officers during the cruise, consisting of papers from my assistant, Lieutenant Wellsted, the late Dr. Hulton, and Messrs. Cruttenden and Smith. It will therefore be evident that Lieutenant Wellsted was only a subordinate officer, acting under obedience to my orders." To emphasise Haines's feelings, Wellsted was not included in any thanks within Haines's own papers, while all other senior personnel were listed. However – as a counterbalance – in his thanks within his *Travels in Arabia* neither did Wellsted include Haines, the pair did not gel.

Before Wellsted's publications, Haines had entrusted him with the leadership of Socotra's land survey and initial negotiations, presumably in Arabic, with Sultan Amar bin Saad bin Tawari. Wellsted appears, in fact, to have deferred to Haines in any decisions he made, even though Haines was absent. Indeed, Wellsted writes explicitly, "My instructions directed me." The glowing reception of Wellsted's publications might have been the cause of Haines's published irritation of 1844.

SOCOTRA BACKGROUND

Geologically, Socotra is a stranded fragment of the ancient supercontinent Gondwana. Its present position arose some 20–15 million years ago, when the opening of the Gulf of Aden detached it from Arabia and left it on the Somali (African) Plate rather than the Arabian one. The island's backbone, the Djebel Haggier (Hajhir/Haggeher Mountains) , is built of Precambrian granitic and metamorphic basement rocks that rise to about 1,500m. These highlands intercept the cooler, wetter winds from roughly November to January; their slopes and upper wadis are used by livestock herders who move up to take advantage of the mist and rain.

Across much of the rest of the island, the basement is mantled by younger limestones and sandstones of Mesozoic and Cenozoic age, especially on the Diksam plateau. Here the landscape is pitted and fissured into karst: caves, sinkholes and dry valleys, many of them noted by Wellsted. Around the margins of the island, narrow coastal plains of alluvium and wind-blown sand fringe the sea. The beaches are often formed of coral and shell-derived sands; their brilliant white gives parts of Socotra a deceptively "tropical atoll" appearance, despite its continental geology.

Socotra's plant life is globally important. Some 835 species of vascular (complex structured) plants have been recorded, of which about 37% are endemic – a level of endemism surpassed only by a handful of other oceanic archipelagos. Iconic species include the dragon's blood tree *Dracaena cinnabari*, with its upturned umbrella crown and blood-red resin; the Socotra bottle tree or desert rose *Adenium obesum* subsp. *socotranum*; the cucumber tree *Dendrosicyos socotranus*, the only tree-sized member of the gourd family; and several endemic frankincense trees *Boswellia* spp., notably *Boswellia socotrana*. Many of these plants store water in their swollen trunks and branches and draw moisture from sea-mist as much as from rain, living, as it were, on the breath of the monsoon.

Frankincense (boswellia sp)

Animals are likewise often unique to the archipelago. Reptiles show especially high endemism, with the Socotran chameleon *Chamaeleo monachus* as a conspicuous example. Among birds there is a small suite of endemics, including the Socotra golden-winged grosbeak *Rhynchostruthus socotranus*, Socotra starling *Onychognathus frater*, Socotra buzzard *Buteo socotraensis* and the locally important seabird Jouanin's petrel *Bulweria fallax*. By contrast, larger native land mammals have vanished and are presumed to have been hunted out in the past. Offshore, fringing and patch reefs host a mixture of Red Sea, western Indian Ocean and wider Indo-Pacific coral and fish species. The surrounding seas hold the non-migratory Arabian Sea population of humpback whale *Megaptera novaeangliae* and several dolphin species, notably Indo-Pacific bottlenose dolphin *Tursiops aduncus* (often seen close inshore), spinner dolphin *Stenella longirostris* and common bottlenose dolphin *Tursiops truncatus*.

Russian fieldwork in 2008–09 reported Oldowan (2.6 and 1.4 million years ago) -type stone tools near Wadi Tharditror in central Socotra and in the Raquf area of the eastern plateau, suggesting that early hominins reached the island during the Lower Palaeolithic. Direct evidence for continuous settlement from that time is lacking, but these finds hint that Socotra's human story may be amongst the world's oldest. By the end of the first century BC, the island was firmly embedded in monsoon trade. The *Periplus of the Erythraean Sea* (first century AD) calls it Dioscorida, describes it as a large island off Arabia near Cape Syagrus (Ras Fartaq) and notes that it "belongs to the king of the frankincense-bearing land" – generally taken to mean the Hadrami kingdom on the adjacent Yemeni coast. Inscriptions in Brahmī, South Arabian, Greek, Palmyrene, Bactrian and other scripts, carved by visiting merchants in Hoq Cave between the first century BC and sixth century AD, underline Socotra's role as a cosmopolitan way-station where traders from all shores of the northern Indian Ocean met. A scattering of Geez script, Ethiopic Semitic, is found on Socotra, including at Hoq cave. By the sixth century AD a Christian community is clearly attested. Cosmas Indicopleustes, the Alexandrian merchant-monk, describes Christians on Socotra, and later sources record bishops of the island subordinate to the Church of the East (often labelled "Nestorian"). In AD 880 an Ethiopian expeditionary force from the Aksumite kingdom conquered Socotra and an Oriental Orthodox bishop was installed, bringing the island for a time under Ethiopian religious and political authority. The Ethiopians were later expelled by an armada dispatched by the Omani imam al-Salt bin Malik (r. 851–885), an episode that shows Socotra already lying within the strategic horizon of Oman.

Much later, from about the fifteenth century, Socotra came under the rule of the Mahrah sultans of Qishn on the Arabian mainland. Their fort and garrison at Suq, then the island's chief port, served to collect tribute and to assert Mahri authority, while day-to-day affairs were left largely in local hands. Under Mahrah rule the population gradually converted from Eastern Christianity to Sunni Islam, though traces of the earlier Christian presence survived in ruins and in local memory into the early modern period.

The Portuguese arrived just as Mahrah power consolidated. Diogo Fernandes Pereira overwintered on the island in 1503, during a voyage before he was connected with the 1503 Armada commanded by Afonso de Albuquerque. In 1507 a fleet under Tristão da Cunha, with Afonso de Albuquerque and Diogo Fernandes Pereira, attacked Suq, stormed the Mahri fort and occupied the island. They converted the captured stronghold into the fortress of São Miguel and briefly attempted to make Socotra a Christian outpost controlling the approach to the Red Sea. Poor soil, lack of reliable fresh water, difficulty in supplying the garrison and disease all undermined the project, and by 1511 the Portuguese had dismantled the fort and abandoned the island. Mahrah control was promptly restored.

Geez script

Although Socotra lay within the wider contest between the Ottoman Empire and its rivals, it was never brought under sustained Ottoman administration and does not appear as a tributary province in Ottoman records. Instead it remained a remote, lightly governed dependency of the Mahrah sultans. That relative autonomy helped to shape the next shock. Around 1800, during the expansion of the first Saudi–Wahhabi state under Amir Abdulaziz bin Mohammed Al Saud (1765–1803), Wahhabi forces from southern Arabia briefly seized Socotra. Naval support came from the Qasimi's in the Persian Gulf. Later accounts, drawing on Vitaly Naumkin's fieldwork, record that they destroyed Christian cemeteries and churches along the coast near Hadibo and tightened control over local Islamic practice – a short-lived intervention, but one that effectively erased most remaining visible traces of the old Nestorian community.

Steam navigation and the Suez–Bombay route then brought Socotra back into British calculations. In 1834 the East India Company stationed a small garrison on the island, which was withdrawn – as above.

Between 10th January – 7th March 1834 Wellsted explored much of Socotra. As its greatest length is just under 134km and surface area less than 3,800km (none too dissimilar to Cyprus) the visit could be done at leisure, and it was. This was partly due to the difficulty of obtaining pack animals and guides and general obstruction by the settled townsmen.

Wellsted described the agriculture and livestock of Socotra in some detail. The soil in places was described as fertile, and he remarked on the livestock in many of the locations he visited. At Cadhoop "herds of cows, and numerous flocks of sheep and goats, were feeding on the luxuriant herbage" and in the sea "fish in this part of the coast are numerous". Water also seemed to be readily available. Notwithstanding all these resources Socotra, at the time Wellsted visited it was, as it is today, a backwater. This despite being astride the exit from the Red Sea, which since antiquity was a major sea route.

Wellsted literally counted the people he met and wrote that they "amounted in all to above two thousand" and based on that he estimated the total population of the country at around 4,000 people. The population was spread over much of the island, in small settlements. The culture and life of the population was continually described "We did not endeavour to conceal our mirth at the appearance of the two gallant candidates for nuptial bliss; they were both verging on seventy, and their wrinkled and decrepit appearance corresponded with their age". He also noted the simple manufacturing undertaken "I found this party busily employed; some of their number were making knives out of part of a hoop which they had procured from some whaler; the anvil was a small piece of iron fixed on a block of wood; the furnace was fed with charcoal; and the combustion was maintained at the requisite intensity by means of a rude pair of bellows, which was constructed of the skins of sheep."

Wellsted seemed very at ease travelling through the entire island, though he had a preference for the rural Bedouins, compared to the coastal "Arabs". The Bedouins after some nervousness on meeting Wellsted treated him very hospitably, and Wellsted and his companion Cruttenden reciprocated when he "perceived that one of them cast an eye of affection on the buttons of his jacket, he accordingly cut one off and presented it to her, after which it became impossible to evade being equally complaisant to her companions; and in the course of a few minutes his jacket was completely stripped, and they as completely satisfied". With the Arabs he "always adopted one plan, which was to laugh outright at it. If, as on the present occasion when they observed the presents which we made to the Bedouins, they afterwards wished to become familiar, I treated them with indifference and neglect; and they then usually left, muttering some expression in the Socotran language."

Wellsted's *Memoir on the Island of Socotra* not only illustrates the island 200 years ago, but is an excellent guide to the nature and culture of it today.

Memoir on the Island of Socotra
Communicated by
Lieut. J. R. Wellsted,
East India Company's Marine Service.
Read the 27th April and 11th May.

CHAPTER I
HADIBU

On the 4th January, 1834, we left the coast of Arabia, and early on the morning of the 10th (after having been becalmed and drifted about by violent currents for several days) we made the island of Socotra. The day was clear and bright, and the whole length of the island was exposed to our view, presenting, to the eastward, a chain of hills of nearly equal height and appearance; to the westward, though more detached, an outline not more remarkable; in the centre, a lofty chain of mountains with their summits yet enveloped in the morning mists. Under the influence of a freshening breeze we rapidly approached the island, and at a distance of about four miles bore away in a direction parallel to its shores. The hills near the beach, and those of which we caught but a transient glance through some opening of the valleys in the interior, were clothed with bushes and trees to their very summits; and their foliage of a lively green had to us, long accustomed to the parched and arid scenery of the Arabian coast, a cheerful and picturesque appearance. We proceeded along till the discovery of some whitened buildings pointed out the position of the town, for which we immediately directed our course; and in a short time we were lying safely at anchor abreast of the houses.

The approach to, and prospect from, the anchorage in the bay of Hadibu (Tamarida) was singularly beautiful and romantic, and was in every way calculated to give a favourable impression of the general fertility of the island. Stretching along the inner extremity of the bay, in a line parallel to, and at a short distance from, the white belt of sand which forms the margin of the sea, a dark line of date trees shows itself detached into three separate groves. Within the western of these, intermingled with the trees, a few of the houses may be perceived, their whitened walls and cottage-like structure giving them a neat and rural appearance. To the left a hill (called by the Arab pilots Djebel Rummel (Djebel Rummel), or the hill of sand), forming the southern and eastern extremity of the bay, is covered on its sea-front, from the base to the summit, by a solid slope of light coloured sand driven up by the force of the northerly monsoon. To the right, steep broken cliffs rise up perpendicularly from the beach, while huge blocks dislodged from their faces lie half immersed at their base, so as to receive the full force of the swell which rolls, chafes, and bursts with great fury against them. But it is to the granite peaks above that the attention is principally directed. These rise immediately over the town in startling abruptness, the steep, sharp, and pointed peaks, which form the upper part of the range, displaying a clear, well-defined and magnificent outline, and assuming a variety of fantastic forms; while in the woody glens that skirt the lower ridges, numerous streams are seen showing out from amidst the clustering foliage, or leaping over the darkened rocks in bright and sparkling cascades. A contrast equally striking and beautiful is shown by the variety of colouring thus produced. The lower ranges, from the luxuriance of the vegetation, and the umbrageous foliage of the trees, have a sombre and shadowy aspect, while the granite, divested to appearance of every particle of vegetation, exhibits on its grey surface, when lighted up by the sun's rays, a variety of veins and patches streaked with brilliant red.

Shortly after the vessel was moored I proceeded to the shore to make the necessary arrangements for a tour through the island. When abreast the town I found a considerable surf, and we therefore pulled up towards the centre date grove, where in a small nook, somewhat sheltered by a projecting reef, we were enabled without much difficulty to effect a landing. Here we were delighted to find a stream about thirty yards in breadth, of which the waters, clear, though shallow, discharge themselves over a sandy and pebbly bed, with much rapidity, into the sea. Numerous palms, enclosures of grain, and plantations of tobacco, with a high luxuriant grass on which numerous flocks of sheep and some fine bullocks were grazing, gave here also great promise of general fertility; and we were well disposed to receive several natives who had watched the approach of the boat to the shore, and now waited to offer their congratulations on our arrival. Under an impression that we were Whalers who had touched at the island for refreshment, we were at first saluted in a curious and not very choice selection of phrases which the natives have gathered from this class of visitors, but when they discovered that several of the party spoke Arabic, they perceived their mistake, and became exceedingly anxious to know who and what we were. We did not, however, evidently to their great disappointment, stay to parley; but, accompanied by the greater number, made the best of our way towards the town, crossing in our progress two other streams equal in width and size to the first, and after passing through a few lanes with detached houses on either side, (having in front small and neat gardens,) we halted near a building somewhat larger than the rest, which our guides pointed out as the habitation of the individual we sought.

During our late survey of the Arabian coast, we had frequent occasion to remark the little state which surrounds the several Arab Chieftains on whom the usages of the country have bestowed the magnificent title of Sultan or king; but notwithstanding our experience, we were scarcely prepared, in the present instance, for either the mode of our reception or the appearance and condition of the individual who received us. After waiting for some time at a low gate, we were admitted into a small court-yard, and were thence conducted into a dark, dirty, and confined room, about eighteen feet long and ten broad, without carpets, mats, or furniture of any description. Here we were joined in a few minutes by a little, bustling, active, old man, who, under the name of Abdallah, announced himself as the person we sought; and to whom, accordingly, after some preliminary observations, I delivered the letter with which I was furnished by the Sultan of Qishn (Kisseen), the acknowledged sovereign of the island, and which directed every assistance to be given us in the prosecution of our inquiries. The old man read this without any comment, and then coolly handed it to his neighbour, who followed his example, and so on until all those who were in the room had become acquainted with its contents. It is a feeling very general throughout the East, and is one which, in the course of our surveys, has given us no small trouble, that the English undertake their costly and extensive surveys, merely that they may obtain possession of the country in which they are conducted with greater facility; and in this instance the injunction contained in the sultan's letter (to conduct us to any part of the island to which we might be desirous of proceeding) appeared so much at variance with the general policy pursued by these chiefs in such matters, that they set it down as a forgery of our own: though of this, as they conversed in the Socotran language, I at the time knew nothing.

After some conversation, I found that camels only were in general use as beasts of burden on the island; and my interpreter, after much wrangling, concluded a bargain for six. [0] I considered everything therefore now arranged; for the two parties, after keeping fast hold of each other's hands, and repeatedly calling on Allah to witness the inviolability with which the compact on either side was to be observed, pronounced the word ' tum,' which on the Arabian coast always terminates a dispute of this nature. Accordingly, after receiving an invitation to pass the period of my stay in Hadibu, in Abdallah's house, I went on board to prepare my baggage; and, before definitively landing, shall now, therefore, give a very brief account of what has hitherto been known of the island, as well as the precise nature of the objects we had in view in at present visiting it.

The island of Socotra, Zocotra, or Socotora, appears to have been known at an early period to the ancient geographers. Ptolemy notices it under the appellation of Dioscoridis Insula, and Arrian says that the inhabitants of it were subject to the kings of the incense country; but from this period it appears to have attracted little attention, and may almost be considered as lost to geography until the visit of Marco Polo in the thirteenth century, who does not, however, make any particular mention of its inhabitants and resources. Vasco de Gama, in his memorable voyage from Lisbon to Calicut, in 1497, passed without seeing it; seven years afterwards it was made known to European navigators by Fernandes Pereira; and Albuquerque at a somewhat later period took possession of it. At the commencement of the seventeenth century, when the increasing spirit of commerce and enterprise led several of our squadrons to enter the ports in the Red Sea, it was frequently visited for shelter or refreshment; and in 1800, when the French army was in Egypt, Commodore Blanket was authorised to take possession of it, but does not appear to have found this necessary or advisable under the circumstances in which he was placed.

Aloe spicata

Notwithstanding these several visits, however, our accounts of the inhabitants, and of the appearance and produce of the island, have been always hitherto vague and contradictory. By one traveller, a Captain Downton, a notice of whose voyage is in my possession, it is stated, "That its chief produce is aloes, though the annual amount does not exceed a ton; that cattle may be bought, but are exceedingly small; that, according to the dry, rocky barrenness of the island, wood is at twelvepence a man's burthen, and every other particular is very dear;" - concluding, "that of stones, arid and bare, the whole island is composed." By another, on the contrary, it is described as a populous, fruitful island, of which "the inhabitants trade to Goa with the produce of the island, viz. fine aloes, frankincense and ambergris, dragon's blood, rice, dates, and coral." Yet, inconsistent as these statements appear, both travellers may have described with fidelity what, at the period of their visit, was presented before them. Independent of the evidence which exists as to the former productiveness of the island, when contrasted with its present state, we must consider that those parts of it which are exposed to the view of passing travellers, are mostly limestone cliffs, of which some portions are indeed covered with a scanty sprinkling of soil, but generally of an inferior quality, and so hard, that the grass which it nourishes dries up almost as soon as the rain ceases which may have caused it to spring forth. The appearance of Hadibu, on our first arrival, as just described, was the consequence of some recent showers of rain; but when I visited the same scene a month afterwards, all was parched and barren, nor did it during our long stay in the SW. monsoon at all improve in its appearance.

More than one vessel has at different periods been despatched to examine the nature of the harbours and anchorages of this island; but, owing to some cause which I cannot explain, our information on these points has not hitherto been superior to that regarding the interior, and our ignorance on both subjects seems the more remarkable, when we consider the position of Socotra, directly in the route of the trade from India by the way of the Red Sea (the entrance to which it may be said to command) on the one hand, and close to the track of our ships by the way of the Cape on the other, - a position, the advantages of which, under an enterprising population and enlightened government, could scarcely have failed at some period to have brought it into great commercial notice and prosperity. For besides this, the trade which is at present centred at Mocha, where ships, from the strength of the southerly winds, are frequently detained four and five months, might be most advantageously removed here, where, though the S.W. monsoon might prevent boats from bringing their cargoes at that time over, it could never prevent ships from touching and taking away merchandise brought by them during the fine season.

It may be observed, also, that these advantages were not overlooked by the Portuguese; and the forts which remain in the vicinity of Hadibu still attest the importance which they attached to its possession.

At the commencement of the present year, various causes combined to render the establishment of a steam-communication between India and Europe an object of general interest and discussion; and the attention of government became thus particularly directed towards Socotra, along the shores of which it was anticipated that some well-sheltered harbours might be discovered, which would serve at all seasons as a coal depot. In order to determine this point our ship (the *Palinurus*) was directed to proceed to the island and commence a survey of its exterior; and while the attention of Captain Haynes in the ship was directed to this object, it was determined that I should proceed towards the interior, in order that I might, from personal observation, report on the various other subjects on which government were desirous of possessing information. All this had, been planned prior to our arrival at the island, so that, having everything in readiness, I returned with my baggage the same evening to the shore. In order to facilitate our progress over the mountains, which were described to me as steep and of difficult ascent, I studiously avoided bringing with me more than I absolutely required, viz. a few changes at linen, some provisions (in case we should find any scarcity on the island), my instruments for celestial and other observations, a small bed which answered also as a saddle (a mode which, by the way, I recommend to all travellers who have occasion to journey on camels), and a small tent which was constructed on board, and considered indispensably necessary in order to shelter us at night from the dew, to which we had reason to believe that exposing ourselves would be found the more injurious, from the quantity of vegetation which we had been assured at Qishn grew in every part of the island. As yet, too, I knew nothing of the character of the people among whom I was about to pass a considerable time; and I was anxious to display nothing that might excite their cupidity: for, as a general remark in all uncivilized countries, it may be observed, that the greater number of accidents which have befallen travellers have arisen from the temptation which has been held out to plunderers by the appearance of much baggage.

At Abdallah's house, in the course of the evening, I received the visits of the principal inhabitants of the town, who were evidently desirous of ascertaining the views of the English with respect to the island. That we should be desirous of obtaining a knowledge of its harbours preparatory to the establishment of steam-navigation, appeared to them in no way surprising "we had, they had heard, been permitted to do so in Mohammed Ali's country: but they could not comprehend how, without some sinister motive, we should voluntarily undergo all the necessary trouble and expense consequent on an examination of the interior; and they neither believed my statements that the Europeans were often induced to do such things for the mere furtherance of science, nor was my intimation that our present journey had for its object the seeking for coal better received. They naturally asked if either that or gold was found (for since they heard that we were anxious to examine the geological structure of the hills, they naturally concluded that we were looking for the precious metals), or if, indeed, any other natural production of value were discovered, it would not form an inducement for us to come and take their island. And I soon perceived that, unless I could remove this impression, there would be little chance of accomplishing the principal objects of my projected tour, for routes that were at first described to me as perfectly practicable, came to be spoken of as destitute of water or wholly impassable; and, notwithstanding their promise of the morning, it was intimated to me before they took their leave that I should not be permitted to proceed in any other direction than by way of the sea-side to Qalansiyah (Colesseah). It was even with difficulty that I obtained a promise of a guide to accompany me in the morning on my visit to the various objects of interest at and about Hadibu.

January 11th.-The following day, accordingly, as I had anticipated, no camels were forthcoming; and the next three days were consumed in negotiating with the Arabs for them, every subterfuge being tried to induce me to forego my demands. But as I was in no hurry, I cared little for all this, and left the ship's interpreter to get over the difficulties in the best way he could, while I passed the time in examining the town and its neighbourhood, of which I shall now give some account.

The nearest range of hills to Hadibu {including those which form the lower ridges or skirts of the granite mountains) approaches the sea in the shape of an arc; on the chord of which, and nearly equidistant from the two points where the extremities reach the beach, is situated the town. It consists at present of about 150 straggling houses, which are all unconnected with each other, and surrounded by date trees; but of this number not a third is now inhabited, the remainder being in the same ruinous and dilapidated state as they were left by the Wahhabis (Wahhabees) in 1801. Though small, they are well constructed of limestone and coral; fragments of the former being found in every part of the island: and the latter abounding near the sea-shore in the vicinity of Hadibu. From its softness it is easily hewn into the required shape from the solid rock, and the natives prefer it thus to the detached pieces which are found along the beach. The houses are usually two stories high, of a square form, and with a tower in one corner, in which the staircase is usually built. Where the rains are so frequent and violent as in Socotra, it becomes necessary to construct habitations of sufficient strength to resist them, and as coral, when exposed to the action of the atmosphere, readily decays under the influence of rain, it is found necessary to cement them, over sides, roofs (which are flat and surrounded with a high parapet), and floors. with a very durable plaster upwards of an inch in thickness. This is also prepared from the coral, the process being simple. The canoes and catamarans bring it to the shore and break it in small pieces, which are piled over lengths of firewood placed across a hollow in the sand. A fire is then placed underneath, and as the lime is calcined it falls into the hole. Where sand is mixed with it, it also answers as mortar. The upper rooms are appropriated to the use of the harem; in the lower, seated on one of the benches, which are usually found on either side of the door, the Arabs receive visitors and transact all their business. The windows face the north-eastward, and are partially closed, like those in Arabia, by a profusion of ornaments in woodwork, through the interstices of which the air and light are admitted. To each house a small garden is attached, in which a sufficiency of beans and melons for the use of the inhabitants is grown. Inclosures of tobacco are also common.

The number of inhabitants at the period of our visit did not exceed a hundred. Several were absent at Zanzibar, but fifty added on that account would include the whole of those who at any period reside here. The Bedouins flock down here from the hills on the arrival of a ship, and their presence may induce a casual visitor to estimate their number higher than I have here done, but I am certain that my estimate is not deficient. There are but two shops in Hadibu, and the only articles exposed for general sale are dates, grain, tobacco, and cloths. Every individual, therefore, on the arrival of a boat, supplies himself with whatever he requires.

In commercial transactions among themselves money is rarely or ever used, and certain quantities of ghee are substituted. Dollars are demanded from strangers visiting the port; and from my party rupees were taken, when they became, from actual trial, assured of their value; but there is no small coin of any description here or on the island. All the silver they obtain in exchange for articles supplied by them is made into ear-rings for their women. Amber and ambergris were both formerly employed as money; but the practice, for some reason with which I am unacquainted, is now discontinued. Both of these substances are occasionally found on the western shores, but I do not think any very considerable quantity is obtained.

Concerning the character, pursuits, &c., of the inhabitants, I shall offer all the necessary information when speaking of the island and its inhabitants in general. The plain, enclosed by the range of mountains already spoken of (at the back of the town), is four miles broad at the widest part, and five miles long. It is watered by three streams (one flowing close past the houses), which at no period are wholly dried up. The water is remarkably pure and light. A line of date trees on either side of these extends from the base of the hills to the sea-shore, where they spread out into large groves. The ground through which they pass is composed of a few sloping hills and rounded hillocks, intersected by plains and small ravines, on which, where destitute of trees and bushes, the glass affords good pasturage for sheep and goats. A singular kind of grass (the *Cenchrus divisus* Wellsted wrote *pennisetum dichotomum*) is found here and in other parts of the island. The stem is about twenty inches in length, and around the upper part a number of radii branch forth, at the extremity of each of which is a sharp-pointed spire or prickle, also barbed. Whenever we dismounted from our camels to walk, we found these a great pest and annoyance, for they adhered in great numbers to our clothes, and frequently penetrated the flesh. Considerable care was also necessary in extracting them, for if they were broken and the barbed parts left in the wound, a painful swelling arose, and they were not removed until suppuration took place and they became by that means ejected. They also adhered with much tenacity to our clothes, from which, when once lodged, it was very difficult to remove them. The soil in some of these plains and valleys is of a reddish-coloured earth, and appears, especially in the vicinity of the date groves, rich and fertile. In others it is of a lighter colour, is filled with small stones, and looks of a poorer quality. With the exception of the palm trees, a few melons, some tobacco, and a few enclosures of pearl millet (*Pennisetum glaucum* Wellsted used the word *dukun*), no part of the plain is cultivated. As I have already noticed, the vegetation near the streams is abundant and luxuriant; but it is the rank luxuriance of a tropical climate unaided by any traces of culture, though grain and vegetables might be cultivated here to any extent, as might also the greater number of inter-tropical fruits. Besides the water supplied by the streams, there is abundance in every part of this plain, few of the wells being of a greater depth than eight feet, and the generality of them not more than five.

I traversed the whole of this ground in search of some remains of the Portuguese; but the only traces I was able to discover were two forts, one situated on the lower ridges of Djebel Rummel, and another on a small rounded hillock in the centre of the plain and nearly abreast of the anchorage, from which it shows very conspicuously. Both are now completely dismantled, and have nothing in their appearance to entitle them to further notice. In the vicinity of the former some groves are pointed out by the Arabs as containing the remains of the *Faringees* (Europeans), and near the small hamlet of Suq (Suk), the remains of a town may be seen, which, under the name of Hadeeboo, tradition says, was the principal one on the island. Beyond the floor and walls of the houses nothing now remains to point it out. I am unable to ascertain at what period Hadibu was erected, but from its name and the appearance of the houses, I am inclined to think it must have been posterior to the first arrival of the Portuguese; and most probably it was erected by those who succeeded them in the government of the island. The natives date its existence from a much earlier period, but little reliance can be placed on their testimony.

Amidst the groves near Suq it is said that considerable quantities of brass are yet occasionally dug up, with hilts of swords and broken fragments of armour. As soon, however, as they are found they are shipped off to Muscat or Zanzibar for sale, [1] and thus, as none were found during my stay, I was unable to procure any. In my search for coins I was equally unsuccessful. Near these ruins there are also a number of Muslim (Musselman) tombs, which consist of small square edifices, with cupolas constructed of earthen pots built over them. The graves are built up in the centre, and cemented to the end of the wall opposite to the door; in one, the natives say that half the body of a celebrated warrior is deposited, the other half being lodged in another about two miles distant. The Wahhabis, however, from the abhorrence with which they regard the erection of edifices over the dead, broke and destroyed the greater number of these, as well as the other tombs which are erected in their vicinity. The latter are met with in every part of the plain; but, as they are constructed of coral, which speedily decays when exposed to a moist atmosphere, the inscriptions were much effaced, and I could find none dated earlier back than 200 years. To return to my Hadibu friends.

CHAPTER 2
DEPARTURE FOR QALANSIYAH

January 13th. - Finding that I was determined to proceed, and fearing the resentment of the English (a feeling which I by no means discouraged) if they still continued their opposition, I was this evening furnished with camels, and told that I might proceed on my journey in any direction which I pleased. My arrangements were soon made, and everything was quickly packed on the camels. The mode in which they arrange the baggage differs here from that generally adopted in Egypt and Arabia. In place of permitting it to hang low on either side as is there customary, they here pile a succession of very thick hair mats over the hump, and along the back, which they bind up by cords passed along outside them into a level ridge somewhat higher than the hump. Long baskets containing the baggage are then placed at the same height on either side of this, and on the top of all were extended our beds; on which, at an elevation of fourteen feet from the ground, we seated ourselves, and set forth on our journey. As I was merely desirous this evening to get clear of the crowd which followed us, I encamped, as soon as they left, in a small shallow valley near a reservoir and some wells, about three-quarters of a mile from the town. My party consisted of Mr. Cruttenden, midshipman; Hamed, our guide; Suleiman, a sort of assistant to him; two slaves to attend the camels. fetch firewood, &c.; a Nubian boy, who attended on Mr. C. and myself; with an Indian as cook, - in all, eight persons.

My instructions directed me to proceed by any route I might deem the most interesting to Qalansiyah, where I was again to meet the *Palinurus*, and receive any further directions which it might be considered advisable or expedient to furnish me with. But as the ship had to survey the intermediate coast lying between the two ports, and consequently would not, it was anticipated, reach the latter harbour before sixteen or eighteen days, I determined, if practicable, to proceed at once into the interior, and, if any road existed, to cross the mountains which were described to me as girting the southern shore, so as to be able, while collecting as much information on my route as practicable, to obtain also a cursory knowledge of the nature of the coast, and the position of the islands which lie contiguous to it. With this view, then, when we had pitched the tent, and were comfortably seated after dinner round a blazing fire, I began to sound our guide respecting the instruction he had received from the chief in Hadibu relative to our journey; and was not much surprised (after the violation of their most solemn promises in the first instance) to find that he was instructed to take me by no other route than that to which I had before so strongly objected, by way of the sea-shore to Qalansiyah. To remonstrate, however, would have been fully as useless as to have returned to Hadibu, and I therefore resolved to remain silent and to proceed by slow stages for the next two or three days, until I could communicate with the ship and inform Captain Haynes how affairs stood. I therefore turned the conversation on other subjects, and we were soon deeply engaged in a dispute respecting the relative merits of the Muslim and Christian creeds. Hamed, our guide, was an intelligent fellow, and was very inquisitive about our religious observances, as well as our mode of praying. The people in Hadibu had already noticed our want of morning and evening adoration; eating pork had also been laid to our charge; so that against the outward semblance of a zealous profession of faith I found it somewhat difficult to defend my position, that the purity of the Christian doctrines, which a Muslim can never appreciate, was, when they were rigidly though silently observed, more than equivalent to them.

January 14th. - This morning we had struck our tent, and were journeying on before sunrise. After riding for about twenty minutes across a plain thickly covered with bushes, we dismounted from our camels for the purpose of walking over a rugged and steep path which leads along the sea-face of a range of hills that rise up without the intervention of any beach almost perpendicularly from the shore. Within and immediately above this a second and higher range rears itself, from the steep and shattered sides of which the action of the elements continues to detach huge masses, some of which appear just arrested in the act of rushing down the steep, and waiting in all probability but the next season to do so, while the weight or impetus of others having overcome every obstacle, they are now lying in scattered fragments in the sea: some of these are of a magnitude so enormous, that they might justly be termed hills, and one, forming a bold promontory projecting out into the sea, was upwards of 150 feet square. A considerable change on this account must be constantly going on in the structure and appearance of this part of the island, while the fury with which the surges lash the shore at this season aids the work of decomposition; and their re-action by carrying off the particles thus abraded from the cliffs (as may be observed) in a muddy stream, adds to the belt of soundings which extends from off the shore. In all probability, this, as well as the

Tihama (Zehama) (coast plain), which bears in its appearance strong evidence of having been formerly covered by the sea, owes its origin, and progressive increase, to the causes which are thus still in full operation. The morning air was keen and cold, and the hills on the left effectually sheltered us from the sun; but the atmosphere in several places received a delightful fragrance from the numerous aromatic flowers which grew around in rich abundance. The road was, however, so bad, that it became a matter of surprise how the camels could pass along it; and in some places it was so narrow and steep, the rock (a compact siliceous limestone) of which it was composed having been also worn smooth by the constant passing of foot-passengers over it, that it was not without difficulty, and in one instance some little danger, that we were able to get our camels over it. From the formation of the feet of these animals, they are but ill adapted to roads of this description, though they proceed over those which are more rugged with as much, if not greater, facility than most other beasts of burden.

Ras Qalansiyah

We next arrived at a pass where the rocks were smooth and rounded, and lay piled one above another in some confusion: over these we scrambled, not without the assistance of our hands, to the top, where we seated ourselves to watch the passage of our camels. Three crossed safely enough, but the fourth slipped at the worst part of the pass, and slid down to some distance, until his progress to destruction was stopped by his inserting the joint of his hinder legs into a hollow, whence he contrived cautiously to regain his footing: a few yards farther, and he would have rolled over the precipice, and been dashed to pieces on the rocks below. I could not but remark, that in such a situation, when the movements of any other animal would by fright have probably hastened its own destruction, those of this camel indicated the most perfect self-possession. But a few yards from this spot I observed the skeletons of two camels which appeared to have shared the fate that our own, in this instance, so narrowly escaped. Here and in several other parts of the road, which are very narrow, the mountains rise up like a wall on the one hand, while there is nothing to prevent the passengers from falling over the precipice on the other; a meeting of two camels on such a spot at night could scarcely fail to be fatal to one, or both. The state of this path exposes a curious trait in the character of the inhabitants: they have built up with much labour such parts of it as may have required slight additions and repairs, while those which are worse, and which but a little larger share of perseverance would have removed altogether, they have left in their original state, wholly untouched. The scenery, however, even where the road is worst, more than compensates for any feelings of insecurity. It blew fresh this morning, and a heavy rolling sea tumbled with much violence on the rocks below us; the roar of the waters, though we were at times elevated about two hundred feet, was almost deafening; the white spray flew to the height of thirty or forty feet; and the surges where the sea encountered the smooth surface of the rock mounted nearly as high; at other places, from its soft and calcareous nature, the incessant action of the waves had sapped many deep subterranean caves and passages, so that when these became filled with some huge wave which burst just without the entrance, the water jetted forth with much violence from the orifices in the upper part. I never witnessed a more magnificent sight than a walk of two hours thus afforded me: at the expiration of that time we arrived at the upper part of a pass, at the foot of which the maritime plain again commences. From hence we saw the village of Qadub (Cadhoop), which is situated on a low piece of land, and is nearly insulated, being partly encompassed, on one side by the sea, and on the other by a deep lagoon: here we halted and took our breakfast. I found a sufficiency of amusement in sketching and describing the trees, collecting plants, &c., until the approach of sunset, when we descended the hill about half way; and inscribed on the soft and yielding bark of a *Camhane* tree (cucumber tree *Dendrosicyos socotranus*), saw some Arabic inscriptions dated as far back as 1640. At the foot of this pass we found several date groves, with some wells and a stream of fresh water; and in a few minutes afterwards we were joined by some Arabs who had seen us descend the pass: with whom we proceeded to the village, where we were shown into a court-yard attached to one of the Arab houses, and there pitched our tent. Few of the Arabs had seen or heard of a Christian before, and our appearance and customs, the various articles of our baggage, and, above all, our astronomical instruments, excited their wonder and astonishment. We sat up conversing, drinking coffee, &c., with them until far after midnight.

Qadup

January 15th. - I rose early this morning, and after strolling over the village and by the sea-side, I walked out into the surrounding country, but such a crowd soon collected, that I found no pleasure in pursuing it, and therefore returned to the tent. The village of Qadub, (Cadhoop or Kathoop), contains thirty houses, and about double that number of huts; the former are smaller than those of Hadibu, and of more rude construction; the latter are miserable hovels, and neither shelter their owners from the wind, the keenness of which at this season is much complained of, nor from the rain. The principal occupation of the inhabitants is either in fishing or in tending their flocks: one member of the family, usually a female, suffices for the latter; and as the boisterous nature of the weather prevents the boats from putting to sea during the greater part of the year, it follows that a very considerable portion of the men's time is passed in idleness. The fish in this part of the coast are numerous, but are not distinguished by any peculiar or superior quality. A moderate-sized *Baghla* (*buggalow*) was lying at anchor in the offing, in which some of the villagers trade to Zanzibar and Muscat. Some traders, who collect ghee from the interior, also reside here, as do several of the husbandmen who tend the neighbouring date groves. Abdallah, in his visit last year, levied a tax of two dollars each from several household proprietors, but many were exempt on the plea of their alleged incompetency to pay. On my return to the tent, I found we had committed a great error in not pitching outside, for, independent of the noxious exhalations which arose from the neighbouring lagoon, and the exceeding closeness and heat of the enclosure, the natives continued to flock in during our stay, and though perfectly civil in their demeanour, yet their constant importunities and queries respecting every article in our possession left us even, during our meals, without a moment to ourselves. In the evening I therefore moved out to the base of the hills at the distance of about half a mile from the village, where we found the ground more elevated and dry; and the mountain air, as it came keen and fresh down the valleys, was an agreeable change from the close, insalubrious atmosphere we had left; we felt the change to be the more sudden and grateful from the absence of our numerous friends, whose curiosity did not so far overcome their natural indolence as to induce them to follow us. Several herds of cows, and numerous flocks of sheep and goats, were feeding on the luxuriant herbage and the numerous aromatic plants which grew in great profusion around us.

A small hamlet had formerly occupied the spot where we had encamped, but nothing more than the ruins of the houses could now be traced. These were not larger in their dimensions than those of Qadub, and otherwise only deserving of remark from a legend which has been preserved, ascribing their erection to the Portuguese. A ruin on the side of the hill, somewhat larger than the others, was pointed out to me as having served to that people the double purpose of a church and fort. As my guide, since our arrival at Qadub, had continued firmly opposed to any deviation from the sea-coast road to Qalansiyah, and neither threats nor promises moved him, and as his influence with the people in this village was too great for me to shake him off and procure another, I was (as it would have been impossible for me to proceed without one) obliged to wait the return of a letter which I contrived to convey privately to Captain Haynes: I therefore passed several days in this delightful spot, wandering over the neighbouring hills, sketching the scenery, collecting plants, &c. On these occasions, to prevent my appearance from alarming the mountaineers, I took with me no other person than an Arab lad as a guide, and the only weapons I carried were a pair of pocket pistols, which were studiously concealed even from him; but notwithstanding these precautions, I found them either so timid or so utterly surprised at the sight of an European, that they invariably fled whenever they saw us approach. In this district, beyond the first range of hills from the sea, there is a sameness in the structure and appearance of the country which leaves but little room for remark; the mountains are compact limestone, differing in no respect from those which I shall have occasion hereafter to notice more fully. In the valleys which intersect them, and which are beds of torrents in the S.W. monsoon, rounded fragments of porphyry, granite, and sienite, which have been washed from the central chasm, are deposited.

January 16th. - I found that our guide this morning had received a letter from Hadibu, and one from Captain Haynes was also brought to me. In this I was informed that on the receipt of mine it was plainly stated by him to the Arabs at

Hadibu, that when they voluntarily engaged their camels for a definite period, with a specified agreement that I was to proceed on them to any part of the island which I pleased, and with that belief, and in earnest of the due fulfilment of my part of the bargain, they had received payment in advance, - they forfeited, by any violation of that agreement, any claim to the indulgence with which he had felt disposed to view their former dislike to my proceeding on the island; and that he should, if any further opposition was offered, take active measures to compel them to perform their part of the compact. The result of this conference was an order from Abdallah to our guide, instructing him to comply in every respect with my wishes. My friend Hamed, therefore, made his appearance at once, and with the most unblushing effrontery retracted all he had said before, acknowledged that the roads were good, that there was an abundance of water, and that I should find no difficulty in proceeding in any direction I wished; in the evening, therefore, not without some regret, we left our encampment and proceeded with our camels along the base of the seaward range of hills. The height of this range averages from 500 to 700 feet: for two-thirds of which they ascend with a gentle slope, and are covered with vegetation and trees; the remainder is mostly bare, and exposes the grey weather-beaten appearance of the limestone worn into numerous caves and hollows. I ascended a hill for the purpose of examining one, but in the first which I came to there were several women and children, who raised such a hideous outcry, and were withal so alarmed at my appearance, that l was too happy to escape the scene and make the best of my way down the hill again. The whole of this range was table-topped, and as we advanced to the westward it gradually retired more towards the interior, while the plain between us and the sea increased its width. The soil of the plain is of an argillaceous nature and reddish colour, mixed in some places with rounded pebbles of augite and silex. Our path lay through a brushwood of Hildebrandt's boxwood (*Buxus hildebrandtii - Metayne*-trees), which grow in some places with a regularity that gives them the appearance of being planted rather by the hand of man than by the caprice of nature: from their height they offer a considerable obstruction to the progress of the camel, as their branches just reach the baggage, and would, were not this strongly and securely packed, soon destroy or remove it; our bedding, which was packed outside, suffered after we had been on the island miserably in these encounters - mine became literally torn to shreds.

Near the beach these bushes disappear, and the plain rises with gentle undulations into rounded hillocks, which are covered with grass of a fine quality, on this several herds of cows and some fine sheep were feeding. Towards the approach of sunset we halted on a small ridge: extending from a hill which stood out on the plain detached from the other mountains. Directly we had pitched our tent, Mr. Cruttenden descended with our guide to a valley below, where we could discern a party of natives driving before them a flock of sheep. The men as usual fled; but some old women made a bold stand, and bitterly reproached Hamed when he drew near for bringing the Europeans over the island. The promise of some grain, the gift of a handkerchief, and the positive, though gratuitous, assurance of our guide that though Europeans we were Muslims, who were on our way to Qalansiyah to join our ship, somewhat pacified them; and after a further conversation of some minutes, they produced an abundant supply of milk, with the promise of a sheep should we require one. I eagerly embraced the opportunity thus afforded me of opening a communication with them, and in addition to what was promised I added some trifling presents of cloths, needles, &c.: these I was happy to perceive had the good effect of creating as much confidence as I could wish or at present desire, for in the evening two young lads were despatched by the party to make whatever observations and inquiries they could: they were fine, intelligent youths, each about sixteen. In answer to several questions which I put to them, they informed me, through our guide, that their friends usually resided on the mountains, but that they had descended with their flocks to enjoy the more abundant pasturage produced by the late rains in the places below, and were now on their return to their native wilds. As I expected to be there too at no very distant period, this encounter was the more fortunate that it would prepare them for our visit; I therefore described myself and companion as proceeding, by direction of the English sultan, in search of coal; that we should pay (a great thing in an eastern country) for whatever we received; that we were, moreover, provided with presents for those who might either behave well to us or assist us in our pursuits; and, above all, I endeavoured to impress on their minds that the natives had not the most remote reason to be apprehensive of us. The lads and old man were now shown the various articles in our tent, to the use or appearance of which they were as utter strangers as the veriest savage in the wilds of New Zealand. Their astonishment was, of course, great; a dark lantern and watch especially attracted their surprise and admiration; a thermometer and the various astronomical instruments excited an equal degree of awe and astonishment, and they could not be prevailed on to touch either one or the other. They remained chatting with us to a very late hour, and then left in high glee on being presented with some other trifles.

It was well we took the precaution of securing our tent before we went to sleep, for the wind blew through the gap in the hills with so much violence, that if we had neglected to have done so we should during the night have stood a fair chance of being blown over the hill.

January 17th. - On the following morning, after breakfast, I visited the Bedouins below; they now testified no alarm at our appearance, and, seated on skins under the shade of a *Ziziphus spina-christi (nebek-*tree - *lotus nebea)*, they quietly awaited our approach; the salutation of peace, " *salaam alicum,*" was exchanged; and we were soon seated in unreserved communication with them.

Ziziphus spina christi

As our guide did not on this occasion accompany me, I was enabled through one of their party who spoke Arabic to obtain a knowledge of some of the roads, which afterwards proved of much service to me. The communication between the Arabs and the Bedouins cannot be very general, for not one in twenty of the latter know anything of the Arabic language; and the proportion of the former who understand the Socotran is scarcely greater. I found this party busily employed; some of their number were making knives out of part of a hoop which they had procured from some whaler; the anvil was a small piece of iron fixed on a block of wood; the furnace was fed with charcoal; and the combustion was maintained at the requisite intensity by means of a rude pair of bellows, which was constructed of the skins of sheep, a tube about six inches in length being attached to the lower part which answered as a nozzle, while at the upper part a small piece of wood served the purpose of a handle, with which a man worked them alternately in a vertical direction. The hoop being cut to the required length, was merely rounded at the extremity, and beaten somewhat thinner on either edge; the lower end was fitted into a haft of the Hildebrandt's boxwood wood, and the operation was then judged to be concluded: deep indentures from the blows of the hammer were visible in those which were handed to me as being finished, but these they told me were left to be removed by constant use. Others were also busily employed tanning skins, to serve for carrying water or milk; for which purpose they use the bark of a tree called *taleo*. The skin is first soaked in it, and afterwards the bark is rubbed in its dry state over it. One of the old ladies who had supplied us with milk the night before, and two of her daughters, had taken up their abode in a natural bower formed by the umbrageous foliage of an *eshaib* tree , at but a short distance from the group with whom we were seated; and the feeling of curiosity, so strongly implanted in the female bosom, predominates, it would appear, fully as much in Socotra as in other parts of the world, for they soon became very solicitous and clamorous to be permitted to join the party, and when denied by the men, contrived to approach with coffee, and under various other pretences, until they had fully satisfied themselves as to our appearance. Latterly, also, following the example of the natives, I entered into conversation with them; and they gave me no reason during the remainder of our stay to complain of either shyness or timidity. From this halting-place I made an excursion to examine some inscriptions which were described to me as having been executed at a very remote period. No water was, however, to be procured here, and it therefore became necessary first to retrace our steps to Qadub. After filling our skins at this village with that necessary, about noon I started on my journey, there was but little wind, and in the valleys and hollows where that little did not reach, the heat was most overpowering. Two miles from Qadub I passed a shallow valley filled with date-trees, which is called Moree (Mori), after the name of the cape to which it is contiguous. In the winter season a rapid stream passes through here, the limits of its bed being prevented from increasing, and thereby injuring the date groves on either side, by walls built along the banks. Numerous huts and a few store-houses are occupied by those who tend the trees; and excellent water, from wells about eight feet in depth, may be procured. Our route hence skirted along a deep bay called Gaobut Kommah. Whenever I left the road for a short time to enjoy the cooler air on the beach, I saw several fragments of red coral, madrepores, and a great variety of shells, among which I noticed a broad belt of white coral extending for several yards into the sea; but neither that nor the shelly limestone with which it is often mixed occurs so frequently, or in the same form, as in the Red Sea, where the latter rises up into hills which extend in some places for several miles along its shores: whereas here I never met it in a larger quantity than an occasional fragment washed up by the surf, nor does the coral, excepting in one instance, (at Ras Moree,) rise up in the reefs and banks which are there so numerous. After leaving Ras Moree, which is a low sandy spot, the Hildebrandt's boxwood -trees disappear, the sandy spaces become more frequent, and are sometimes covered for a distance of several yards with a saline incrustation.

Continuing our ride for a couple of hours more we arrived at some curious inscriptions. They are cut in the horizontal face of a sheet of limestone rock, which is on a level with the plain and about 300 paces in circumference. Those parts, which by their smoothness are best adapted for the purpose, are covered with inscriptions and figures. The resemblance of the characters to some which I copied at Wajh (Wedgee), on the coast of Arabia, and supposed to be Ethiopic, is so striking, that I am inclined to think that they owe their origin to the same people. Should this resemblance, on further examination, prove not imaginary, some very interesting inquiries will naturally suggest themselves. Independent of these inscriptions there are a vast number of rude representations of the feet of men, camels, sheep, oxen, &c.: some as small as those of an infant, while others are treble the natural size; they are all placed in pairs, but with no general direction; the feet of the animals are cut so as to represent a soft rock yielding to the weight of their impression: they occur sometimes in a line, sometimes thickly crowded together; and amidst the latter are usually found the characters. The cross occurs very frequently, as well as a figure with a snake's head. I passed several hours in examining and sketching the most legible, but vast numbers have been obliterated. I was at first inclined to ascribe these inscriptions to the work of shepherds in their leisure hours; but they are so numerous, and from the nature of the rock must have been executed with so much labour, that I cannot, on reflection, refer them to that origin. The unity of design, exhibited in the constant recurrence of the same apparently unintelligible symbol, would rather induce us to suppose that a place of worship, or pilgrimage, must have formerly existed in this vicinity. At present there are half-a-dozen small ruinous buildings to the S.E., and the remains of a wall running along to the N. near it; but nothing more to verify such a supposition.

In the evening we again left our encampment, and proceeded by a road to the southward of, that by which we had passed the day before. Our path now lay along the base of a range of hills which forms the exterior chain on this side of the island; it is frequently broken by transverse valleys into detached masses, and along the base of these in the winter are formed very rapid streams. The sea-face of these hills is very precipitous, but they appear to slope away with a gradual descent towards the interior. Their general outline and appearance continues otherwise similar to those described already; their direction is here W.S.W.; and though they dip at various directions, yet from 20° to 25° with the horizon is the usual average. Numerous trees, shrubs, and wild flowers, the latter at this season in full bloom, give to the scene a picturesque appearance which it did not possess at a later period when I visited it; but as we advance the plain becomes again barren and sterile; along the sea-shore the bushes disappear, and are exchanged for extensive sandy tracts; neither habitations nor sheep are visible, and only a few wretched-looking goats occasionally crossed our path. Shortly after sunset we encamped under some *Ziziphus spina-christi* - trees at the entrance of the valley by which we, the following day, were to pass into the interior. There we were very fortunate in falling in with a large party of Arabs who were preparing a marriage feast; - two sheep cut into small pieces and boiled in an earthen pot, some rice, a few onions and some excellent dates, formed the meal to which we were invited and gladly sat down. We did not endeavour to conceal our mirth at the appearance of the two gallant candidates for nuptial bliss; they were both verging on seventy, and their wrinkled and decrepit appearance corresponded with their age, they bore the numerous jokes of the party, however, on the event with much equanimity [2] - the oldest of the brides was not, I was assured, more than seventeen, and the sum paid to the parents was ten dollars. It has been advanced as an argument for the wisdom of Mahomed's permission to the *Muslim* to engage a plurality of wives, that females decay more rapidly in the east than males - that a girl 15 is married at thirteen - is a mother and in her prime at fifteen - and is faded at twenty-five; while the vigour of the male, excepting (as is not unfrequent) in cases of excessive sensual indulgence, continues unimpaired, it is pretended, for the same period as in a more northern clime.

As spirituous liquors appear unknown on the island, our meal was quickly concluded, and after the necessary ablutions had been hastened over, we adjourned to another tree underneath which them was a small portion of greensward. There, to my great surprise, I found the party had assembled for the purpose of dancing. In Arabia it would be thought unbecoming for an Arab to play on any musical instrument, and far more so for him to engage in dancing; on this account I expressed my surprise to an old man standing by me, at finding the present group thus employed; he, however, denied that any island Arabs were mixed with them, and assured me, if I thought proper to inquire, that I should find that all who were there were natives of the hills. I thought this was not strictly speaking true, yet the greater number were highlanders who, probably from living in a milder climate, and a more invigorating atmosphere, are by no means averse to such amusements. In this instance they were unprovided with any musical instruments, and one of their number was compelled to chaunt a tune while the others occasionally joined in chorus. To this rude tune a number kept a sort of time by a succession of rude jumps or bounds, without any pretence to regularity of step; while the others stood round in a circle, clapping to the tune at the same time with their hands. In this manner they amused themselves until midnight, when the bridegrooms took their leave and joined their fair partners who were staying with their parents among the hills. In return for the hearty welcome which we had received, it was of course impossible to remunerate them in any other way than by a small present, without giving them offence; and I therefore felt much pleasure in an early part of the evening in being able to add to the mirth of the party, by supplying them with a little tobacco, of which they are passionately fond. We had several heavy showers during the night, but the tent effectually sheltered us; our slaves were also offered a berth inside, but they preferred remaining outside wrapped in their thick mats, which they use in the daytime for putting over their camels.

We left early the next morning, still continuing our route along the base of the same hills; and after two hours' ride over the same barren tract as before, we entered the opening and found it to be a broad valley, the bed of a torrent: the water could only have retired lately, for the heat of the sun had split the mud into clefts and crevices. The plain extends with a moderate and gradual slope to this point, and from its elevation we were enabled to observe, that it is stony in some places and sandy in others; a few scattered and dwarfish bushes occur occasionally along the banks of the torrents by which it is intersected. Bounding this plain, and extending from the sea in a direction nearly at right angles to that which we had hitherto skirted, another range takes its rise near the sea, where it forms a bluff, and runs at an elevation of 1100 feet for several miles towards the interior, where it constitutes the western side of the valley along which we were now travelling. Numerous *eshaib*, *Ziziphus spina-christi* , and Socotran Pomegranate, (*Punica protopunica* – Wellsted used - *ukshare* (wild grape)) trees line the road on either side, and under the grateful shade afforded by one of the first we halted to breakfast. A female who passed a few minutes afterwards, sent us, unsolicited, a large bowl of milk, but she would not approach the party though I sent to ask her to do so. She was accompanied by two little boys, who had their mouths and nostrils covered with a small square piece of cloth, to protect them, I was told, from a species of tick which infest the sheep, and which, if they obtain a lodgment in those parts, produce violent inflammation and are difficult to extract.

Our camels having browsed for some time on the tender branches of the *Ziziphus spina-christi* , we again started about noon on our journey. Continuing to follow the bed of the stream, we crossed a uniform tract of rounded masses of limestone of various sizes, and as the road wound a good deal our progress was but slow. We passed several pools of fresh water deposited in the sides of the valley, from the last of which, near the termination of the valley, the country opens, becomes more fertile, and its aspect is consequently more cheerful; we then crossed a plain two miles and a half in width, covered with thick grass on which numerous flocks of sheep and goats were feeding. At five o'clock we entered another narrow valley, which we continued to ascend until it was nearly dusk, when we pitched our tent under the shelter afforded by some *Ziziphus spina-christi* trees. Before us, I was much gratified to find several of the cavernous habitations I have before taken notice of. The same present which we received in the morning was again sent to us, and I afterwards observed that it became a general practice for the Bedouins to do so whenever we halted. During the night the wind blew in powerful gusts, dense clouds passed over the face of the heavens, the rain descended with the full force of a tropical shower, we had much forked lightning, and the thunder as it rolled amidst the distant mountains was awfully sublime. The natives were much terrified by the lightning, and entreated us to withdraw from beneath the trees, several of which, at but a short distance from us, had at a former season been struck by it. However, as it was here more elevated and dry, and was, moreover, somewhat sheltered from the rain, I did not adopt their advice; in the morning several trees were shown us which had suffered in the way they described.

As the weather continued gloomy with slight showers, I determined to pass the day here. After breakfast I walked up to the caves, but they were, in consequence of the rain, so crowded with sheep and goats, and, moreover, so infested with vermin, that I felt but little inclination to remain for the purpose of examining them very minutely. The only natives I found in addition to those who visited us overnight, were some aged females busily employed in weaving: their loom was very rude. Two young lads were employed in making butter, by shaking the cream in skins: while the older were repairing a strong but light net, which is used for catching the wild goats. The nature of the rock in which these caves are found differs in no respect from the limestone which occurs so generally in other parts of the island; but they differ greatly in height, depth, and general outline, from each other, though such as me best adapted for the purpose appear to have been occupied at various periods as habitations. I looked in vain for any stalactitical remains or formations - large rounded masses, having numerous small cells (occupied by pigeons and several other kinds of birds, which have taken up their abode there without fear of molestation from the natives), was the general appearance of the surface of the interior. The whole was stained with a reddish-coloured clay, containing particles of iron, which traverses the interior of the rock in thin and narrow veins. From this it also occasionally receives a reddish brown, and also a purple or iodine- coloured tint, which contrasts in some instances, in a most singular manner, with the dark-coloured vegetation clustering in thick masses around. By one of those changes which appear not less frequent here than they are in the variable atmosphere of our native clime, the heavy and dense masses of clouds floated away, the rain ceased to fall, and in a few minutes the sun burst forth and lighted up a sky of that deep and cloudless blue, which is probably never seen but within the tropics. The bed of the river (where we were encamped) appears to be never perfectly dry. In it I found rounded masses of limestone and sienite; there are also scattered fragments of porphyritic, sienitic, and common grey granite, the rocks from which they have been detached apparently passing into each other. In the latter, the mica prevails in rather large leaves, and the hornblende is light coloured and scarce, in the porphyry the crystallizations are very coarse, and the grains easily separated. Wherever the torrents have exposed the soil on the bank, it appears of a reddish colour, with small rounded pebbles of limestone and petrosilex embedded in it; the descent of the stream is very rapid, and some of the fragments are upwards of four feet in diameter. They are all rounded by the attrition consequent on their progress, and are so numerous that they form a complete layer from bank to bank; the width is about two hundred yards, and it may be considered as the principal stream on this side of the island, for there is only one nearly as large running along the base of

Fadan Matallah. It is only during the latter part of the S.W. monsoon that these and the other streams on this side of the island fill their beds; but they do this then so copiously and with so much rapidity, that they are, at this distance from their embouchure into the sea, said not to be fordable even by camels; we had before us even now sufficient indication of the strength of the current in the numerous trees that had been torn up by the roots, and carried to some distance, until an inequality in the ground had again arrested their progress. These were principally *Ziziphus spina-christi* trees, which, along the borders, and in the centre of the stream, were particularly numerous. From the door of my tent I counted in one direction twenty-seven, some very large and all thickly covered with fruit. This tree is well known to botanists as the Ziziphus spina-christi-its height is usually from twenty to thirty feet--the bark is light-coloured, rough, and crossed longitudinally by numerous fissures; the leaves are cordiform (or heart-shaped) and small, the branches are large, but the foliage is somewhat scanty. Notwithstanding the hardness and length of the spines which grow on its branches, intermingled with its leaves, the camels, from the cartilaginous formation of their mouths, feed on both with much avidity, and without to appearance suffering any inconvenience. The fruit, of which they are equally fond, clusters in great abundance amidst its branches, and from its golden colour gives to the tree a rich and pleasing appearance, the natives assert that it is produced at all seasons; it resembles a cherry in form and size, and has a peculiar though mild and pleasant flavour. The Arabs pound them between two stones into a paste-like consistence, which they mix with ghee, and swallow with much apparent relish.

Accompanied by one of the Bedouins from the caves, in the evening I scrambled up the hill. At the summit I found an extensive natural reservoir of rain water, which was described to me as being sufficiently capacious to supply the inhabitants and their flocks for an extent of several miles; on its bank numerous *eshaib* and *Ziziphus spina-christi* trees were growing, and a vast number of rock pigeons and other birds, attracted here by the water, were fluttering amidst their branches. A party of highlanders with their camels had halted here; but after repeated attempts I found their reluctance to enter into conversation with us was too strong to be overcome. From this point I obtained a complete view of this part of the island; but as the map and other data which accompany it will yield every necessary degree of information, and a further detail of the local features of this part of the country would offer but little if any interest, I shall forbear further topographical reference at present, - merely observing, that between the first or leeward range, along which our route skirted, and another which is higher, and lines the southern shores of the island, there is a broad plain or rather valley, which is crossed by traces of torrents in all directions: along one of the most considerable of which, extending in a S.E. direction, lies our route to-morrow, and near the point where this issues from a deep cleft in the mountain we are to commence our ascent.

January 18th. - This morning, after packing up, we proceeded, therefore, in a S.

E. direction across the plain, and passed several Bedouins and Arabs, who cheerfully returned our salutation of peace; some of the females fled at our approach, though I observed one who stopped and testified her respect to us, after the Arabian fashion, by squatting down and turning her back towards us. The plain appeared stony, and though occasional patches of verdure occurred, yet they were neither extensive nor numerous, and the general appearance was coarse and barren. A few *Ziziphus spina-christi* and some other trees lined the sides of the streams; half a dozen hamlets and some few solitary houses appeared at scattered distances, and the large flocks of sheep and goats which were perceived feeding around were tended by Bedouins from the hills, who towards the evening drove them up to their caves in the mountains, a few head of horned cattle, and here and there a stray camel, mingled curiously in the scene. Towards noon, we halted in a narrow stony valley, at the foot of the pass; the width of this plain was eight miles. Close to where we encamped there were some enormous masses of pudding-stone, composed of the same rounded materials which I have enumerated as being found in the streams. My stages in this part were purposely made short, as, while this gave me an opportunity of completing a more correct survey of the country, it also enabled me to do away with the unfavourable Impression with which the inhabitants were disposed to view us, and to cultivate by every opportunity their good will and acquaintance, by which I acquired facilities of ascertaining their actual condition and habits. We had passing showers throughout this day, but as they were not very violent, I wandered with my gun for some distance through the valleys and over the lower ranges of the hills. I passed numerous flocks of sheep and goats, and occasionally at a distance a man and woman tending them. Had they seen me they would have fled immediately and spread an alarm, I did not therefore attempt to approach them. The soil on the hills was very scanty - its nature somewhat argillaceous, for in those parts where the rain had lodged, a thin clay coating was formed in the clefts and hollows; a few bushes, some grass, and occasionally a patch of wild flowers were visible; several large trees common to other parts of the island were also found here, among the most remarkable of which was the *Socotran Pomegranate*, or wild grape; about five miles from our tent, I found, for the first time since leaving Qadub, a copious spring of fresh water. It gushed out in a clear full stream from the rock at the Inner extremity of a cave, and after running for about a hundred yards was lost in the sand. I did not find any one here, but the well-trodden paths leading to it in all directions denoted numerous visitors. My guide afterwards assured me that this spring flows in undiminished quantity throughout the year, an invaluable blessing in a district where the only water otherwise obtained is procured from the precarious and uncertain supply collected in natural reservoirs. A few minutes after my return to the tent, first one, and then several Bedouins were perceived looking at us from the summit of a hill; on which our guide recommended that we should conceal ourselves within it, while he, accompanied by one of the slaves, would endeavour to bring them to us. Near dusk he returned with the whole party; a tall man about thirty, who was easily recognised as one of the rulers or elders, seated himself at our invitation in the tent, while the remainder squatted themselves down near the door outside: our new visitor was at first too much astonished at all he saw to trouble himself with any inquiries as to the nature of our visit; repeated exclamations of astonishment burst from him, as be inspected with a hurried and almost childish curiosity the articles we had with us: he was sorely puzzled with the watch, and appeared to believe, with all his attendants, that the beating of the second hand was produced by a living animal. The instant I perceived their curiosity in some measure satiated, I invited him and all his followers to partake of a meal of rice and ghee which our slaves had prepared. The avidity with which they all helped themselves to this, and the enormous quantities which they devoured, verified our guide's remark, that it was but seldom they partook of such fare; and also showed us how far the keenness of the mountain air enabled our guests to excel what, in voracity, I thought the unequalled performances of our attendants. I have remarked that the Arabs (especially those who reside in towns) are by no means so abstemious as they are usually supposed; and the Indian, it is well known, though he indulges in but two meals a day, makes up in quantity for the meagre quality of his food; but I never was more astonished than by the performance of these islanders. The best attempts of the two former are mere pigmy efforts, contrasted with the gigantic capacity of the latter. On more than one occasion, I have seen three of the party which accompanied us finish between sunrise and sunset the whole carcase, head, entrails, &c., of a sheep; and whenever they could obtain them, they would make four meals of animal food during the day, and urge no objection to partaking of whatever rice came in their way between whiles. Nothing excited more astonishment with them than our, comparatively speaking, spare and meagre diet. "That a meal!" said Abdallah to me, one day, in his house at Hadibu, as he observed our servant placing a breakfast for myself and Mr. Cruttenden before us, " why the youngest of my children " (a boy about eight years of age) " devours daily at each meal twice that quantity!" Some coffee and tobacco distributed to them after they were seated put the whole party in the utmost good humour. They conversed with us freely on every subject connected with their customs and mode of life, nor did they feel any reluctance to converse on the subject of their women, in praise of the beauty and fairness of whom they were very lavish. My request for a guide on the following morning was urged at this moment, and to my great surprise, I found no objections were offered; under all the circumstances of the case, this was more than I could have dared to hope for. Hamed, under the plea that it would have drawn down on him the ill-will of the Bedouins, had refused to take me farther than where we were encamped. The pass over the mountains was impracticable for camels, and to have proceeded alone and on foot without them, uncertain of what reception we might have met with from the wild tribes (of whom we knew absolutely nothing) who inhabit their fastnesses, would have been hazardous and unpleasant: yet this I had resolved to do, if Hamed had continued refractory; and our falling in with these men rendered us quite independent of him.

Rain continued to fall without intermission during the night, but as our tent was pitched under a huge impending rock, the whole party were enabled, with the assistance of a blazing fire, to sleep well sheltered and comfortable around us. Towards the morning the clouds rolled away and it became more moderate: we sat up smoking and chatting to a very late hour.

January 19th. - Leaving our tent in charge of a servant, we set out early this morning, accompanied by our new guide, to commence our ascent up the face of the hill; and after an hour's creeping rather than walking, for the bushes prevented us, excepting in clear spaces, from standing upright, we reached the summit of the ridge. The morning mists had not yet cleared away, and our view was consequently very limited; we could, however, discover that the top of the hill was not a level platform, as we had, judging from its unbroken appearance below, hitherto supposed it to be; but was, on the contrary, a pile of mountains of nearly equal height, which were partially divided from each other by narrow deep glens and ravines; none of which, however, completely divided the ridge, or, indeed, indented it to a greater depth than half its width. The bushes which we found so thickly interwoven on the side of the hill disappear at the summit. The trees are few and dwarfish, and occur but at scattered distances. The rock, whitened by the rains, shows itself grey, bleak, and wasted, in all directions. From the same cause its surface is worn into irregular cells and cavities of unequal depth and form, with narrow ridges running between them, so sharp-pointed and rugged, that, even with our shoes on, we found it painful to traverse them; but the natives, accustomed to them from their earliest youth, proceeded with the same facility as we should have done over a macadamized road; and our staggering gait in such places afforded them a good deal of amusement. Several of these cavities from the late rains were now filled with water. After crossing some ravines, which offer, in the depth and richness of their soil, and in the abundance and luxuriance of their vegetation, a singular and beautiful contrast to the summits, we arrived at one considerably larger and deeper than the rest, in which, after we had descended for some time, we found ourselves unexpectedly at the entrance of an extensive cavern, where some females and their children were assembled: the latter gazed at us some time between fear and astonishment, and then ran screaming away; the former seemed inclined to follow the example, until a few words from our guide re-assured them. They still continued for some time to express the extremity of their surprise and astonishment, by uttering the monosyllable - Ha! ha! ha! ha! repeated with much celerity. But our guide shortly explained who we were, and while he was busily employed in driving out the goats and sheep to make a clear space for us to sit down, seeing that we were much heated from our walk, one of the females went out for a few minutes and returned with a large bowl of milk. One of these females was aged, but the other two were remarkably fair and pretty.

They wore no veils, nor did they make any attempt to conceal their faces. In their ears they had a profusion of earrings, and strings of dollars were suspended round their necks: their dress was coarse and rude: a few presents of cotton, needles, &c., which I presented to them in return for their hospitality, operated like magic in removing any former shyness or fear: shortly after this several other females entered, and in a few minutes we were surrounded by about a dozen, who became very importunate and clamorous for some more of the articles which I had first produced. All the stock I brought with me was soon exhausted; and I know not how we should have pacified them, had not Mr. Cruttenden perceived that one of them cast an eye of affection on the buttons of his jacket, he accordingly cut one off and presented it to her, after which it became impossible to evade being equally complaisant to her companions; and in the course of a few minutes his jacket was completely stripped, and they as completely satisfied. Notwithstanding their eagerness to possess these articles, so much good humour and good feeling were apparent in all I saw here, that I determined to make this, if possible, my headquarters for the time I remained on the hills; and I therefore desired our guide, who spoke the Socotran language with facility, to propose it to them. I had taken the precaution to bring the few trifling things we required with us, so that I was fully prepared for the ready assent which was immediately with great glee given to my proposal. We were now, as they explained it to us, as one of the family, and no objections were consequently made to my proceeding to any part of the cave. I found it to be 120 paces in length, and the width and height, though the form was irregular, corresponded with this. The entrance was nearly blocked up by a huge overhanging rock, which excluded the rain, while it preserved the interior from the heat of the sun's rays. Circular stone walls with low narrow doors divided the interior into different apartments, each of which appeared to be occupied by the same family: the number here was eight, and if we give four as the average of each family, it makes forty inhabitants in this lonely recess amidst the mountain wilds. After purchasing a couple of sheep, which I desired might be cooked and eaten among the Bedouins who were present, I left Mr. Cruttenden to keep them in good humour, while I with the guide again set forward to obtain a view of some islands which, together with the sea, I was told I should be enabled to discern from the summit of a neighbouring hill. After crossing several ravines, I came to a small hamlet consisting of but a few huts, which were occupied by some shepherds. As I approached, no men appeared, but the women came out and insisted on my remaining until the youngest of the party should proceed to fetch some milk; when she was absent for this purpose, the companion asked me with much simplicity if I had come on the hills for the purpose of procuring a wife. I laughed heartily at the supposition, and denied that such was at present my intention, for I was not, until afterwards informed of the circumstance, aware that it was quite customary for the Arabs and others who visit Socotra, to proceed to the hills and there seek a partner agreeable to their wishes; from eight to fifteen dollars is the sum usually paid by the suitor to the parents, a much larger sum being, however, demanded should the girl be particularly useful or beautiful. These huts were constructed with loose stones, and thatched with *cadjans* (date palm leaf), but otherwise differed in no respect from those which will be found described hereafter. A few yards from them was an enclosure for sheep. After quitting this hamlet we followed a rocky path along the edge of a ravine, until we arrived at the extremity of the range, which terminates in an abrupt perpendicular precipice. Along the face of this, a few feet below, there is a step or stair-like projection, about two feet in width, which answers as a terrace and pathway to a number of caves ranged like cells in the rock. In order to prevent their cattle and children from falling over the profound precipice below, the shepherds who inhabit them have erected at the anterior part a narrow wall, but notwithstanding this, a more tremendous habitation in the S.W. monsoon time can scarcely be imagined. The extreme haziness of the weather prevented my seeing the island of Abd al Kuri (Abdul Curia), and it was even with difficulty that I was enabled to discern the island of Samhah (Sanchar). The Tihama or mountain plain below us was here intersected by numerous traces of torrents from the hills: there seemed an abundance of grass bushes and dwarfish trees. This mural precipice extends parallel to the sea-beach for several miles; and unlike the cliffs on the N.E. side, which are clothed with vegetation, this is in some places entirely bare, and the rain has given it the same worn, weather-beaten, and grey appearance, which I have before noticed, while in others it has a dark and gloomy look. Having made all necessary observations, I returned shortly after noon to the cave, when I found the whole of its inmates busily employed dressing the sheep, a small part of which served for our evening meal; and having procured some grass which was strewn on the rocky floor, we wrapped ourselves up in our boatcloaks, and fatigued with the events of the day were soon asleep. But our slumbers, it was destined, should not be unbroken, for towards midnight the rain returned with redoubled violence, and the sheep and goats collected in the cave from all quarters. The noise they made would alone have been quite sufficient to wake us; but not content with this, they continued (attracted by the grass on which we were lying) to run over us during the remainder of the night. To the natives who were sleeping behind in skins they appeared to give no molestation; they continued their slumber with much tranquillity.

January 20th. - We set out early this morning in a S.E. direction to another part of the hill, but met with nothing of interest.' The country was precisely of the same description as that over which we passed the day before, though it appeared more thickly peopled. We passed or entered several caves, which were occupied, and some huts, a few of which occurred singly, but they were more generally found in clusters of from five to eight. I made to-day some splendid additions to my plants, but the only birds I could discover were two more varieties of the vulture, and one which the natives call *arooab* (Socotra Starling *Onychognathus frater*) , the plumage of which resembles that of an English blackbird.

Ras Summare lagoon Qalansiyah

Towards sunset I retraced my steps to the cave, where I found, with the addition of a few to their number, the same party that were present the previous night. Before we had completed our evening meal it was quite dark, and as the atmosphere was keen and cold we found a fire almost indispensable; abundance of fuel was at hand, and we soon had a blazing one before us; as the flame rose red and flickering and in fantastic wreaths to the roof, it lighted up a wild and singular scene. The irregular and rugged outline and surface of the projecting masses in the interior of the cave, stood forth in bold relief, while the lofty, arched roof, and the numerous caverns and other parts more retiring and remote, Were lost in the deepest gloom. The appearance of so many half-naked men with their platted hair, their uncouth gestures, and their peculiarly marked and expressive countenances, were also in savage keeping with the rest of the picture. As soon as we had joined their circle round the fire, we were saluted with a host of questions respecting the domestic life and manners of the Europeans; many of their questions on this and other points displayed great discernment, as well as considerable quickness in understanding the answers returned to them. They spoke of its being probable that the Sultan of Qishn (Kisheen) would dispose of the island to the English, without expressing any surprise or betraying any aversion to such a change of masters. The fame of our Indian government, through the traders who occasionally resort here, had reached even this remote spot. "Should the English take possession of the island," said an old man, "we should at least have a government, at present we have none." I repeated to him our fable of the frogs who petitioned for a king, and afterwards exchanged their log monarch for one of more activity and energy; they were highly, amused at the application. They maintained an interesting conversation respecting their habits and mode of life until a late hour. I may, however, remark here, that in order to avoid the repetition which would attend a continued insertion of disjointed and scattered notices on these subjects, in the order in which they came to me, I have deemed it better to condense them into the general remarks which will be found at the end of this paper. Towards midnight the party broke up; they retired to their skins, which form all their bedding, and we to a ledge on the rocks out of the track of the sheep, where, notwithstanding our indifferent lodging, we wrapped ourselves up in our cloaks and slept soundly until the following morning.

January 21st. - At daylight we took leave of our hospitable friends, and accompanied by one of their number, descended the hill to our tents; we found that the Bedouins in our absence had regularly supplied our servants with milk, and that not the slightest molestation had been offered to any one. When I returned to Hadibu some weeks afterwards, the Arabs there expressed much surprise at the unlimited confidence which we on this occasion reposed in the Bedouins. As Christians and strangers they were surprised that we should have ventured without any precaution at once among a race who were almost ignorant of the existence of Europeans, and of whose habits and character we were equally uninformed. But I found them on our first interview, to appearance, hospitable and inoffensive and cautiously abstained on that and on every other occasion from an unnecessary display of apprehension or precaution which might, by creating distrust, have changed those impressions. Had they at any time contemplated theft or personal violence, I am by no means certain but that from our fire-arms, notwithstanding their numerical superiority, we should, had the attack been open, have possessed the advantage. Shortly after noon we again mounted our camels to cross the island, and after a brisk ride: of thee hours, we encamped at our former halting place, under the *Ziziphus spina-christi* trees, at Makkan Al Shiebah. The night was clear and cloudless, and was the first we had passed on the island without an occasional shower of rain.

January 22nd. - The following morning we again resumed our journey by the same road by which we had arrived, until we attained the termination of the valley, whence we struck off to the westward by a path about a mile to the south ward of Ras Kadannah, for Qalansiyah. A continued succession of large tabular masses of limestone presented themselves for some distance, nor are the flowers and shrubs, as well as the small trees, which find nourishment in the hollows, either of sufficient magnitude or number to change the arid and barren appearance of the scene. But after travelling on for some distance the face of the country improves; grass and trees again clothe the face of the hills, and sheep and goats are found grazing in the valleys. At sunset we halted under a large hill at but a short distance from a hamlet; several Bedouins visited us in the evening. I never saw delight more strongly expressed on a person's countenance than one of these exhibited, when he was shown his cave, through my telescope, at some distance up the hill. Notwithstanding the exuberant vegetation, we found this an uncomfortable halting place, for the flies, ticks, &c., were so numerous during the night, that I got but little sleep. Near this spot I found some fragments of crystals. It took us three-quarters of an hour on the following morning to descend the pass between the range on which we had pitched our tent and Qalansiyah.

January 23rd. - At twenty minutes past ten we left the foot of the pass; our route lay, for about twenty minutes, along the bed of a stream of fresh water; it then loses itself in the sand. My guides informed me that the large pools which are deposited in the vicinity of Qalansiyah, even in the dry season, are filled by this stream. Continuing to wind along the bed of this, we passed over a bushy plain, or rather broad valley, which is formed on the one hand by a range of hills, 1200 feet in height, rising up from the sea, and on the other, by a still higher range, of which, however, more anon. Shortly after noon we arrived at the village of Qalansiyah, which, it will be seen by the map (as Collesseah), is situated at the gorge of this valley; a few wretched houses, some *Date palm leaf* huts, and a small building which serves as a mosque, constitute the village. The inhabitants appear wretchedly poor, and their number does not exceed fifty families. They have a few fishing-boats, which also serve for watering the ships that put in here. That which we obtained was brought from a pool abreast the village, which, as I have noticed above, is fed by the stream, which, in the S.W. monsoon, falls here into the sea; a bar of sand, eight or ten paces in breadth, separates the fresh water from the salt. The water we obtained was to appearance good when it was first received on board; yet, in the course of a few weeks (though kept in iron tanks, which have generally the good effect of purifying it from all deleterious matter), it acquired an exceedingly unpleasant taste and smell. A few fowls and some wretched sheep may occasionally be procured here, but no other supplies of any description. Dragon's Blood, aloes, and ghee, are also shipped in small quantities to the *Baghlas* which put in here. The intercourse with the English and other foreigners does not appear to have worked any very favourable change in the manners and behaviour of the Arabs at Qalansiyah; with their own class they bear the character of being bigoted, selfish, and avaricious to a proverb. I have heard it remarked by our seamen, that when they have asked for a draught of water it has been refused, without some money or a present previously given. Having now procured the few remaining articles which I required from the ship, and received my final instructions with regard to our future rendezvous, I came on shore early in the morning to settle the route by which I was to leave this. I was of course anxious, in order that I might see as much of the country as possible, not to return by that along which I came; and it was, therefore, with much satisfaction that I found my guide and camel-drivers, after much opposition, agree to attempt the ascent of the mountains on the western side, by a track up which, I had been previously informed, the camel-drivers sometimes, though very rarely, have been known to take their camels to pasture. The perpendicular elevation of the part of the precipice over which this path led, was ascertained, by a trigonometrical admeasurement, to be 1900 feet; neither myself nor any one on board had hitherto believed it practicable. Prior to making the attempt, it would, however, I was told, be necessary that the camels should be unloaded at the foot of the pass, and I was therefore compelled to hire men for the purpose of carrying our baggage up: they were not, procured without some difficulty, and it may perhaps serve to show the relative value of money and labour, if I state, that after demanding most exorbitant sums, eight dollars was the least they would take for carrying the few articles we required to the summit of the mountains.[3]

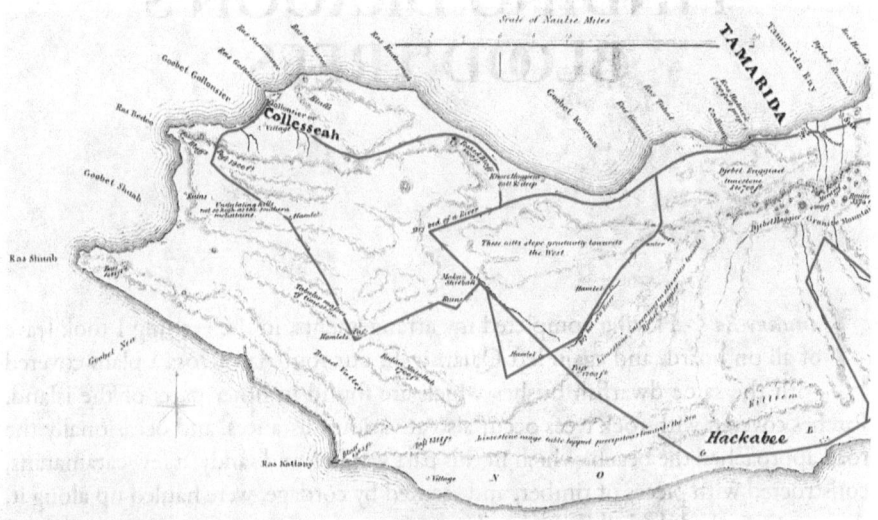

Western Socotra - Wellsteds Route

CHAPTER 3
FINDING DRAGON'S BLOOD TREES

January 24th - Having completed my arrangements, in the evening I took leave of all on board, and again left Qalansiyah: our route lay across a plain covered with the same dwarfish bushes which are found in other parts of the island. Patches covered with rock trees occur also at various distances, and occasionally the road approached the beach, which in this part was low and sandy; a few catamarans, constructed with pieces of timber, and secured by cordage, were hauled up along it. As we approached the hills, we passed several streams running from them; at one of which we filled our water-skins, and towards sunset halted at their base, near a singular perforated mass of rock, which had, at no very distant period, been detached from some part of their sides. As we expected the Bedouins, who were to remove our baggage, towards midnight, we did not pitch our tent, but took up our quarters under the lee of this rock; and after our evening meal, we spread our boat-cloaks on the grass, and with the blue vault of heaven for our canopy, were soon asleep.

January 25th. - We awoke this morning and found that our guide, with the Bedouins, had taken up everything during the night; so we prepared to follow them directly, hoping that some one would make his appearance to point out the path, for in the bold and magnificent rampart before us the eye sought in vain for some track by which a precipice so inaccessible to look at could be scaled. Its surface, in many places, exposed a variety of hollows, some of which, it was evident from the light-coloured tracks that led towards them, served as places of shelter for the shepherds; others had a stair-like appearance; and the plants and shrubs nourished by their soil, and lodged by the rains, gave these rocks an appearance of stratification, which they have not in reality. But our attention was called from the contemplation of these objects by the arrival of our guides, with whom we now set out. The road wound a great deal at first, and the vegetation as we ascended was abundant, the variety of plants and flowers being very great, of which some were highly aromatic.

Goat Skins for Water

We halted, after an hour's ascent, on a hill somewhat detached from the face of the cliff. The soil here was a dark, rich, vegetable mould, six or seven feet in depth, which nourishes several large trees, and among others, the *bohain*, resembling our English sycamore in the form of the leaf and the distribution of its branches;-the *eshaib*, having an equal likeness to our weeping ash;-the *tuk*, a species of wild fig, and many more. From our halting-place, the remainder of the pass was so exceedingly steep, that unless I had perceived the camels following at no great distance below, I could not have believed it possible for them to have accomplished the ascent. I was now, therefore, no ways surprised at the opposition I had met with from the camel drivers. In some places the footpath, barely a foot in width, ran along the ridges which we had observed below, approaching their extremity at times so closely, that but a few inches were left between the feet of the passenger, and the profound precipice that sunk perpendicularly seven or eight hundred feet below him. A false step here (and in some places the rock was worn so smooth that we were compelled to take off our shoes while crossing them) would have been fatal. Notwithstanding the difficulties of the way, the natives followed or preceded us with our various articles of baggage strapped to their backs, without suffering, to appearance, any inconvenience from the dangers or difficulties of the road. After upwards of an hour's fatiguing ascent, we reached the summit, where we were agreeably surprised to find that the country differed not only in climate, but in appearance and produce, from that which we had left.

The barren and sandy track below was exchanged for verdant plains, with gently undulating hills and sloping plains. The thermometer, which stood at upwards of 80° on the plain below, rose outside our tent no higher than 67°. But it was to the scene below that our attention was principally directed, a more beautiful one could scarcely be imagined. From the great altitude we had attained, everything was spread out in beautiful detail at our feet. The day was bright and serene, the sun had reached the meridian, and lighted up all around with splendour. Below, a fresh breeze was sweeping along; yet the vast expanse of ocean-with its horizon elevated to nearly the same apparent level as ourselves, appeared silent and tranquil, its surface, with the exception of a silvery line of surge, which rippled and glistened along the white beach, being wholly unruffled; while many and beautiful hues were reflected from its party-coloured coral, sandy, or dark rocky bottom, all blending, from a lively green into a bright purple, and that again fading away in the distance to a vapour-like blue, which rendered it difficult to distinguish sea from sky. And some boats, which at the instant pushed off from the ship under sail, and our *Baghla* then beating into the bay, with their white canvass, the village of Qalansiyah, its palm trees, and lakes of fresh water, all added to, or lightened the picture.

As I intended to pass some days in this neighbourhood, I sought out a convenient and picturesque spot under some trees, where we collected our baggage, and towards sunset pitched our tent. The evening air was keen and cold, and a fire was very comfortable, while, as we partook of our evening meal by its light, we could not avoid contrasting our present mode of life with our usual cooped up residence on board ship. Some privations we certainly experienced in the absence of what are usually styled comforts; but these are probably necessary to give to the wanderer's taste its true zest, and to balance against them, we had, as Robinson Crusoe would have placed them, the following advantages, which those who have passed many months at sea in a small vessel, in a tropical climate, will know how to appreciate. We were nowise hurried or tied to time, and could consequently halt In those places which we found from scenery or other causes the most pleasant. We had the selection of our own route. We found an abundant and delightful source of amusement in wandering throughout the day, sketching the country and its productions; and we returned in the evening fully prepared for our evening meal. The climate was cool and salubrious,- the natives were as yet well disposed towards us; we were well supplied with every necessary, in a word, we had everything which could render our tour at once pleasing and interesting.

January 26th. - The atmosphere this morning was delightfully clear, pure, and invigorating, and we commenced our survey of the country at an early hour. We first crossed a valley about two miles in width, and then commenced the ascent of a range of hills about 500 feet in height, which extends parallel to those we ascended yesterday. In this valley the soil consists of the same reddish coloured earth before noticed, excepting in some places where the decayed vegetation has changed it to a darker hue or more loamy consistence. In other places the surface is strewn with stones, which are not however imbedded to any depth, and might, with little difficulty, be removed. The grass, for an extent of several miles, is as thick and high as in an English meadow, and would make capital hay, did the natives think of applying it to such a purpose. They do not even, as is customary in most parts under the tropics, burn what remains at the close of the season; and on this account they miss the excellent manure thereby procured for the crop of next season. The whole of this valley, for an extent of several miles, appears thus in a high degree susceptible of cultivation - nor need want of water prevent this. There are indeed neither wells nor running streams, and whether water might be obtained in wells by digging remains yet to be ascertained, as the natives have not attempted to do so; but it is very certain that by means of reservoirs or tanks a sufficiency might be procured not only for their personal wants but also in any requisite quantity to irrigate the ground. From the elevation of this ridge showers are frequent and plentiful, and nothing more would be requisite than to deepen a few of the numerous hollows which abound, and cut channels from various directions to lead to them. Tanks constructed in this manner in Arabia and Persia are frequently filled in a single day. The want of frequent showers of rain, should any be felt here, must be amply compensated by the dews at night, which descend very copiously, insomuch that we found our tent every morning completely saturated by them, while their crystal drops hung: on every surrounding bush or tree. Cottages, numerous inhabitants, extensive flocks of sheep, and some oxen, were met here. The outline of the hills before us was rounded, but still the bare rock protruded its sharp ridges in all directions, from between the crevices of which numerous sweet-scented herbs spring forth, on which the sheep feed in preference to the luxuriant grass below. In my progress across the plain I met with several habitations underground, none of which, however, appeared at present to be occupied. An hour's brisk walking along the ridge of hills, which, at an elevation of about 500 feet, bounds this plain, brought us to its western extremity, whence we obtained a good view of the west or wintering bay, and also an extensive prospect of this side of the island. The map and sketch which accompany these remarks will however render any minute topographical detail unnecessary. No other hills intervene between the point on which we now stood and the west end of the island, which terminates in a profound precipice. Casting my eyes over the prospect to the south-westward, all appeared more wild, dreary, and inhospitable than any other part of the island; the general appearance of the nearer ridges was grey and bare, not however without an occasional dark green spot of verdure.

January 28th. - Early this morning we started. Our route lay to the south-eastward, winding, as we advanced, more to the eastward. The valley continued filled with beautiful grass for a distance of three miles, and after that it became more stony with less verdure. The sheep were very numerous. Shortly after noon we halted at a small hamlet, as my guide maintained that beyond that no water for a considerable distance was to be found. From the tent we saw several inhabitants who, in the first instance, hid themselves on our approach, but finding that we made no attempt, after halting, to visit them, they came, though with much apparent caution and timidity, towards us. Each brought a small offering of milk, dates, or butter; and I gave them in exchange a few scissors, a little thread, and needles. Some small silver coins were also offered them, but they appeared to care but little for them: a few clasp-knives to the men were most acceptable, and both sexes soon crowded round our tent in great numbers. On learning that we were provided with medicines the applications for them were at first incessant: the men complained principally of impotency, and the females of sterility, though, judging from the numerous progeny around us, neither would appear to prevail to any alarming extent. As I had to take some angles and altitudes where we halted, I was obliged to produce my sextant, which, to my great horror, underwent a minute and close examination, but the astonishment with which they viewed so complicated a machine was quite tame compared with the intense and excessive surprise with which they regarded the inverting telescope. I made one of the servants stand at a short distance from the tent while they looked at him through it, for not one of them would, on any account, subject themselves to such a scrutiny-the females, in particular, ran away directly it was proposed to them. It was now, it must be remembered, the Ramadan, and the approach of sunset relieved us for a short time from our visitors, but as soon as they had finished their evening meal a number returned. The greater proportion of these were females, the most noisy and talkative of our former visitors. Numerous and incessant were the questions which they proposed to us: Had we any sheep, goats, or bullocks in our country? Any rain? Did we ever *sully* (pray)? What number of wives had the English sultan? Were we married? But beyond all, and they were joined in this by the men, what were we doing here, "writing down" (as they had seen us) hills, trees, and flowers? This point was the only one on which we found it difficult to satisfy them. They laughed at the idea that the English sultan would be at the expense of sending a ship to " measure the island," or to ascertain in what respect its productions differed from others. "You want to take possession of it as your forefathers the Europeans did," was all I could get in reply to this. The stature of the men we saw here was generally tall, and their figures were well knit and symmetrically proportioned. The same varieties which I have before noticed In their modes of dressing the hair exist here; their eyes are sparkling and lively; the teeth, even of those advanced in years, were of a pearly whiteness; and the expression of their countenances was good humoured, animated, and intelligent. They evinced no jealousy of their women, who, in their turn, after their first introduction to us, as I have already noticed, evinced neither fear nor shyness; several of them were remarkably fair and pretty, with mostly the Jewish cast of countenance.

During the time that the Bedouins were absent at their evening meal I walked to the top of a neighbouring hill, for the purpose of taking some bearings, and making other observations. My station was on the brow of a precipice, 600 feet in height, facing the north. A valley, parallel to the one we were encamped in, ran along the base of this, beyond which, at the distance of three miles, another range, similar to this, rose up with its precipice facing the sea, forming the outer or seaward barrier of the mountains.

January 29th. - When we left this morning, the whole of the party came out to bid us farewell: we also received every assistance from them in packing our camels, and parted with mutual good wishes. For a distance of four miles the road led over a stony level, from which we descended by a very steep path, which was too bad, for some distance, for us to ride. We halted near noon in a broad rocky valley, where I obtained an observation for the latitude; and towards evening we again proceeded. The country, as we advanced in this direction, gradually became more rocky and barren. Our route next lay over similar tabular masses of limestone to those I noticed on our route to Qalansiyah; but in place of the soil in the hollows nourishing the bushes which are there common, I found here only the aloe plant, but that more abundant than in any other part of the island. At four o'clock we arrived at the verge of a pass, and after three-quarters of an hour's steep descent reached the bottom. Along the greater part of the route the stones were removed from the path on either side, so as to leave a broad space resembling a road; and a wall was constructed with them on both sides. The natives attribute this work to the Portuguese, and assert that they intended to make a road along here (i.e. between Hadibu and Qalansiyah); but this is an imaginary legend, as I subsequently discovered that similar constructions were to be met with In many other parts of the island, and served as boundaries to the aloe grounds.

We halted at the foot of this pass, about a mile to the north-ward of a high mountain called Fadan Matallah. On its sides and ravines there is excellent pasturage, and the Bedouins were consequently very numerous. Near the summit on the eastern side there is, as I was informed, an extensive natural reservoir of water, which at no season dries wholly up. The aloe plants are there also particularly numerous, and with my glass too I could distinguish many Dragon's Blood trees. Close to where we halted there was a deserted hamlet, its former tenants having gone with their flocks to the mountains. During our journey through the day we passed several parties proceeding for a similar purpose.

January 30th. -Pursuing our journey to the S. E. we this morning passed some arid and, stony plains in which a few sheep were grazing, and, after three hours travel, stopped at a small building which Is said to have been used formerly as a place of worship. It was, however, impossible, from its present dilapidated state, to pronounce how far this story was true. The ruin is eighteen feet long, by fifteen broad; and on one side the walls appeared to have been carried to the height of thirty feet. They are all constructed of the loose stones everywhere strewn around, and though now divested of mortar, are put together with more care than I have elsewhere observed in any buildings on the island. The length of the building is in the direction E. and W., and it is surrounded by a circular wall, also of loose stones, with four dwarfish doors. All the natives I conversed with on the subject were unanimous in representing it as having been formerly a place of worship, but I looked round on the walls in vain for crosses or any inscriptions. I have understood that a kind of litholatry prevailed here before the introduction of the Islamic (Mahommedan) religion, and one stone of an oblong shape, shattered in three pieces, and bearing some faint traces of having been covered with a red pigment, was pointed out to me; but there was nothing beyond its having received its shape from the hand of man, and its colouring, to warrant a conclusion that it had ever served a religious purpose.

We left this in the evening, and after again descending a small pass found the face of the country much improved, grass appearing and becoming more abundant as we advanced, until we approached our old station under the *Ziziphus spina-christi* trees, at Makkan Al Shiebah. I was desirous of reaching Hadibu by another route than that by which I arrived on the former occasion, but I found our guide Hamed so complete a bar to our progress in any direction from the beaten track, that I now determined to get rid of him at all risks. I detected him here endeavouring to defraud a Bedouin out of money which my servant had given him to pay for some sheep which he had purchased. I had frequently before, on other occasions, found him misinterpreting our communications, as well as making statements that were calculated to create the most erroneous impressions regarding our visit and views on the island, and to which their natural suspicions but too readily induced them to give credit. From the influence which he possessed over the minds of the inhabitants at Qadub, Qalansiyah, and in the western parts of the island, I thought that it would have been impolitic, if not impracticable, to discharge him there; but as we approached Hadibu his influence ceased; and for some days past I had, unknown to him, been treating with young Suleiman, who made me acquainted with several roads which Hamed had declared to be impracticable, and who expressed the utmost willingness to accompany me. Hamed had received pay to a considerable amount in advance, but I willingly relinquished that, (as indeed I had repeatedly on the same conditions offered to do before,) provided he would leave me. For some time he declared his intention to follow me, whether I pleased it or not, but a threat that he at last extorted from me, that if he presumed to do so I would inflict severe personal chastisement on him, had the desired effect; and, providing him with a camel, we now succeeded in persuading him to depart for his house in Hadibu. We found our old friends here very happy to see us, and we remained making short excursions in every direction, though without observing anything of interest until

Civet

February 2nd, when, shortly after noon, we struck our tent, and speedily emerged from the hills, entering on the same extensive plain which we had before crossed. For a short time we also followed the same path; but then struck suddenly off to the E.N.E. The same bare rock continued to show itself above ground, though a great many sheep and goats were browsing on the scanty herbage. About midway across we passed two Bedouin villages, each containing about twenty houses; but we saw none of the inhabitants. Towards evening we entered the bed of a torrent, the face of the country continuing still more sterile and stony. At one of the angles formed by a sharp bend of the stream, the side of the bank was laid bare for a depth of twenty feet, and exposed a reddish coloured soil, with rounded masses and pebbles of limestone embedded in it. Towards sunset we halted on the banks of a small stream, now dry, which is connected with the one we left at Makhan ul Shiebah. The country now became very hilly, but the appearance and direction of the mountains did not differ from those before described. Their general elevation above the plain was about four hundred feet; they are intersected by numerous steep and narrow valleys, and some few expose the limestone rock in a state of stratification resembling a brick wall, each stratum being broken at short intervals not much longer than a brick, but somewhat thicker. Both hills and valleys are covered as before with dwarfish and stunted bushes and trees. It appeared singular, considering the scantiness of the soil, that the roots of all the plants found here were long and tapering rather than creeping. The bushes, and in some places the surface of the ground for some distance, were covered with small shells. A few yards from where we encamped, the natives had dug to the depth of twenty or thirty feet for water, but apparently without success. In the evening we heard the cry of several civet cats close to the tent, and also the screech of a bird called *maleiarid*, at which the natives appear much alarmed. They call it *sheitan,* or the devil, and fling stones in the direction whence the cry proceeds. I was never so fortunate as to obtain a sight of this bird, but from the description of the natives I should judge it to be a species of bat, a supposition which Is rendered the more probable from their having a tale respecting its propensities, similar to that which is told of the vampire bat. During the night we had occasional showers of rain.

February 3rd. - The day was walm, with passing clouds. In the morning the thermometer stood at 75°, at noon it was 80°. Last night we were cautioned by our guide to keep a good look-out for our baggage, as the inhabitants of this district are reputed to possess habits at variance with the general honesty of those in other parts of Socotra; but we saw no one, though there were numerous flocks of sheep and goats browsing around, and last night was accordingly the first evening we had passed on the island without being able to procure the usual supplies. In the afternoon we travelled in an easterly direction for two hours, winding up a valley which is the bed of a torrent. We passed many Bedouins' caves, and saw a great many of their females, though but few of the men. Vegetation here almost entirely left us, but towards evening some grassy patches again appeared, and some variety of trees and bushes remained. Near our halting-place at sunset we found above ten different kinds. Twenty or thirty Bedouins approached us here. Our guide informed me, from what he had overheard, that these men were not well-inclined towards us, and should not be trusted. I thought it as well, therefore, to take the first opportunity of showing them that we were not unprovided with the means of defence, and as, a short time afterwards, one of them put the question direct to me, in what way we should be able to punish those who might feel disposed to pilfer from us, I pointed out a tree at a considerable distance, and asked them if they thought it possible for me to strike it with one of my double-barrelled pistols, which I usually wore hidden at my belt. A smile of incredulity passed over the very handsome face of one of the men who was standing next me, and who had been the most importunate in his inquiries. I immediately drew one of them, and by a lucky chance sent both balls directly through its trunk. More than half their number ran directly the piece was fired, and I never saw greater astonishment than was depicted in the countenances of those who remained; the suddenness of the act, and the absence to them of any visible means by which the powder had been ignited, together with the celerity with which the balls had been discharged one after the other, were so unlike what they had ever seen or heard of before, that they appeared, as they probed the perforations with their finger to assure themselves that it had actually penetrated, to be scarcely able to believe the evidence of their senses. To improve on their present astonishment, our guide, unknown to me, represented to them that if any one, not belonging to our own party, should approach our tent unbidden, they would go off by themselves and shoot them. I should not have ventured to repeat so ridiculous a story had I not been assured by irrefragable proofs that it was circulated with great rapidity over the island, and that to the extent of this credulity we were indebted (especially in the eastern parts of the island) for the safety of our baggage, as well as our not meeting with any resistance while passing through these narrow ravines, where a few resolute men might defend themselves against any force that could be brought against them. The men we saw here were equally handsome and well-formed with the other Bedouins we have met with.

Wadi Dirhur

Shortly after we had halted, I accompanied our guide to a natural reservoir of water, which had been widened and otherwise enlarged by artificial means. It was 340 paces in circumference, and appeared also of corresponding depth; the sides and bottom are lined with stones placed together with much care. I learn that it is not frequently dried up at any season; but when it is, the distress which is thereby occasioned in the immediate neighbourhood is very great, as the next nearest reservoir is that at Makkan Al Shiebah. By deepening or covering this over, so as to prevent the escape of the immense quantity which is now carried off by evaporation, such an event at any season would probably be prevented; but when did an Arab undertake a task with a view to prospective improvement? Around, and on the sides of the tanks, there are a great variety of pendulous or creeping plants, but no traces of cultivation.

While at this station, some matter having formed in the hinder feet of one of the camels, the Arabs effected its discharge in a very characteristic manner. After securing its legs and head, to prevent its kicking or biting, they turned the animal over on its side. The irons which had been made red-hot were then produced, and thrust successively to the depth of three or four inches into the ball of the foot; the animal roared and struggled very much, and its agonies were prolonged to an unnecessary degree by the unskilfulness of the operators, who did not think the operation complete until they had thrust the iron five or six times into the foot, and as a finish had marked across the surface several transverse bars. A halt at least might have been thought necessary to complete the cure; but no, that was quite unnecessary. "He will go better," said young Suleiman, as I stood watching the limping of the poor beast, " He will go better when he warms;" and the remark was made in the same indifferent tone and manner that a hackney coachman on a similar occasion might have assumed.

February 4th. - 7 A.M. ther. 70°, sky cloudy, air cool and refreshing. After a meridian observation of the sun we resumed our journey, and at first wound round the base of the hill which forms the northern side of the valley; after arriving at the termination of which we ascended another range to the right. The limestone shown along the road is here worn so smooth at the surface, that the camels made their way over it with much difficulty, stumbling and staggering at each step. We saw some females on the road, who no sooner perceived us than they screamed out, " Weillah! Weillah! Weillah!" and with the utmost precipitation those who had children placed them either on their backs or under their arms. I was amused by observing one who, finding that her lower habiliments somewhat impeded her progress, threw them, without any apparent hesitation, over her head, and was thereby enabled greatly to accelerate her pace; on another occasion, a day or two previous to this, I observed a Socotran dame similarly situated divest herself of her lower garments in a still less ceremonious manner, for quietly loosening the cameline (which is all they wear below the waist) from her girdle, she dropped it on the ground and fled with redoubled speed without it.

Tamerind (Tamarindus indica)

Their legs, compared with those of the men, appear in some cases to be of an astonishing thickness, and nature, in that part which particularly attracts our attention in the Hottentot ladies, appears in some instances here to be not less bountiful.

After passing several rocky ridges, we next reached the first or outer range of mountains on the northern side of the island; and commenced descending a pass which leads from the summit of this to the plain below. It was steep, and in some places, where the rock had been much worn, very slippery. A large bay, Goobet Koorma, was before us. The granite peaks covered with a purple tinge were on our left, and the plain, torn by numerous torrents looking like white veins on a darkened surface, was below us. As we descended (the pass has a descent of 1500 feet) we found a considerable change In the atmosphere, the heat at the base of these bills and across the plain being very great. At five o'clock we halted at a former encampment; but the Bedouins were now amidst the hills.

February 5th. - I took a drawing of the entrance to this valley with the granite peaks in the background. After completing it we proceeded, our progress continually intercepted by large masses of granite, over which the camels were led with the utmost difficulty: scattered *amaro*-trees occurred frequently; when their branches are broken, they smell strongly of turpentine, but the camels are, notwithstanding, exceedingly fond of them. Not a hut or native did we see in the course of our journey; and the silence, depopulation, and romantic solitude through which we slowly and with difficulty wound our way, strongly reminded me of the wild and savage glens in the vicinity of Mount Sinai. We continued advancing until the magnitude of the masses in our path compelled us to halt about half a mile from the base of the granite mountains: we pitched our tent under the widespreading branches of a tamarind tree, having a beautiful stream gently murmuring over the rocks, at a few yards distance from our door. I seated myself on a rock to enjoy the scene before me, which was singularly wild and magnificent; we had, as it were, penetrated into the heart of a mass of mountains, and pitched our tents nearly in the centre of an enormous and superb amphitheatre, two miles in diameter. The lower part of the range is composed of limestone, feldspar, and porphyry, through which granite spires protrude themselves, grey, steep, and towering to a great height; but by far the most singular appearance was presented by fragments of the lower formations, which were perceived borne up between two superior peaks, or wrapped, as it were, round the shoulders of the higher. The line of junction between the granite and limestone was beautifully exposed to view from this station: it was elevated 3000 feet above where we stood. A short distance to the right was one of the most magnificent and extensive caverns to be found on the island; its length was 250 yards, breadth at its greatest depth 175, and height 87 yards. Within, the interior masses of rock hung, as it were, suspended in the act of falling from the roof; and at the entrance, in the very centre, the arch drooped and rested on a rude sort of pillar: the dimensions and form of this vast cavern were in accordance with the solitary magnificence of the whole scene.

Date Palms and Dragons Blood on plateau Firman

About a mile to the left was a small date-grove belonging to the people of Hadibu, who repair here in the date season to dispose of the produce of their grove. No one is left to take care of the property at other seasons; yet I was confidently assured that neither the fruit nor the *date palm leafs* (the decayed branches, which are nearly as valuable as the fruit) are at any time stolen. All the inhabitants we saw here, men, women, and children, ran directly they saw us. Our servant Sunday, a Nubian boy dressed in European clothes, came close on one of them unexpectedly; and had he been his Satanic Majesty himself, whom without doubt he was considered to resemble, more alarm could not have been shown, or more celerity in escaping. The terrified Bedouin sprang from rock to rock up a nearly vertical hill with almost incredible speed; and so much afraid were they all afterwards of approaching us, that during the whole of the next day they would not bring their sheep to water at the pool near which we were encamped, though it was evident, as our guide pointed out, that they had been in the habit of doing so daily before. A great many wild goats were seen here, and I was able to get sufficiently close to discharge my gun at one, though not fortunate enough to bring him down.

February 6th. - This morning we made an attempt to scale the hills; but, after ascending about 2500 feet, we came to a nearly vertical escarpment, and were obliged to halt. From this point we had a good view of this part of the country. I had before been somewhat surprised at the apparent strength of the torrent along the bed of which we had brought our camels; but from this height I could perceive that several tributary streams led down to it, one passing through thick woods and coming from the northward, while another ran down from the southward. My companion, with the guide, had gone some distance to the right, and I was seated, with my back against a rock, sketching a dragon's-blood tree, of which there were a great number around, when three or four Bedouins made their appearance suddenly before me. I had already picked up some few words of their language, and immediately addressed them with some encouraging expressions. They appeared at first much astonished, and their demeanour was at first so suspicious that I quietly and unobservedly placed my hand on my pistol; but, after the interchange of a few sentences, they seated themselves beside me. A little tobacco, a knife, and some beads, confirmed their confidence, and I had full leisure to examine my new acquaintances. Their only dress was a girdle of cloth bound round their waist; while their hair hung in loose ringlets over their shoulders; and their whole appearance was in keeping with the scene of savage wildness around. It was difficult to survey either without feelings of great interest. This romantic country and its untutored tenants have now for ages remained in entire seclusion, and we were the first Europeans who had penetrated thus far within the recesses of this island, at least for some centuries. The result to these children of nature remains yet to be seen.

Diksam Plateau, Djebel Haggier (Haggier Mountains)

CHAPTER 4
RETURN TO HADIBU

February 7*th*. - Early in the morning we struck our tent, and retraced our steps along the valley by Qadub, and by the pass between that and Hadibu, which, however, now displayed none of those beauties which so attracted our attention on our first visit. Towards evening we reached Hadibu. On my arrival we proceeded to Abdallah's house, who greeted us with much apparent kindness; but we had not been seated many minutes before he presented us with a letter he had just received from an Arab Chief, named Hamed ben Tary, who had arrived some days before at Qalansiyah, and was now employed levying whatever sums he could collect there. In this precious document Abdallah was informed that our researches in the interior were perfectly unauthorised by, and perfectly unknown to, the Sultan, who had indeed given us permission to examine if the ports of Hadibu or Qalansiyah would answer as a coal depot; but nothing more. Almost all the inhabitants of Hadibu soon flocked accordingly to see and question us respecting our journey; and their former suspicion, that the letter we brought was a forgery, was now fixed beyond a doubt. No arguments of mine, at such a moment, were therefore of any avail, or produced any effect in removing their suspicions: I did not, consequently, long persevere in the attempt, but forthwith wrote to Hamed ben Tary, stating the nature of my authority from the Sultan, and that, having received the sanction of the superior chiefs, I could neither imagine (nor would my government suffer) the interference of any inferior; therefore should any further obstacle be placed in our way by him, that our government, as well as his own, would hold him strictly answerable for it. This letter I dispatched by a messenger the same evening.

After their first surprise, for two or three days the Arabs behaved very well; but I found that their visits at last occupied so much of our time that I was obliged to direct they should only be admitted at certain times. They took great umbrage at this, it being, as they asserted, totally at variance with the Arab customs. I however contented myself with telling them that the contrary was against ours; and they became more reconciled to it. I passed the greater part of the day in transcribing my journal, in the evening we walked down to the sea beach, the Arabs not allowing us to proceed in any other direction. Even to an Arab, the swarms of flies during the day, and the vermin at night, must have rendered such a residence unpleasant enough; but to us, who had for some time been enjoying the pure mountain air, it was intolerable, and I began to look for the arrival of our messenger with no small degree of impatience. He arrived at last on the morning of the 10th, and the answer was, "that Hamed ben Tary saw no reason to alter his former directions, and that if we wished to proceed in our examination of the island the ship must again proceed to Qishn, and solicit there the permission of the Sultan to do so: until that should arrive, we were to be confined to Hadibu;" and after dictating this letter, it was further intimated that: he took his departure with the view of proceeding, himself, to the Arabian coast. This was carrying matters with a high band; and had I not known that avarice in an Arab will predominate over fear, I should have despaired of effecting our object. I was persuaded, however, that after a little time our difficulties would be again removed: and meantime I shall notice what occurred in the town.

February 10th. - This evening completed the full period of the Ramadan; but, to the great grief of the most zealous of the *Muslims*, the atmosphere proved so cloudy that they were unable to distinguish the moon, and they refused in consequence to consider the fast concluded. The greater number, however, were not so fastidious, and passed the night in the customary feasting and rejoicings. All the muskets and pistols they had in the town were put in requisition, and fired as long as their ammunition lasted; their houses were lighted up with all the lamps, lanterns, and torches they could muster: large bonfires were made, and some rude fireworks from Muscat were let off. The slaves partook of their amusements, and continued singing, dancing, and clapping their hands, until day--light the next day.

February 11. - All were this morning attired in their best clothes, and the men, moreover, had all the arms they could muster, of whatever description, hung about their persons; men and women were seen chattering and laughing, and apparently enjoying a degree of freedom unknown at other times; all work was suspended, even the slaves obtained a holiday, and large parties of Bedouins traversed the streets, receiving presents of rice, &c., from the town's-people. Sometimes these parties advanced in line, at others two-by-two, dancing, singing, and flourishing the clubs which they usually carry in their hands. After breakfast a procession visited Abdallah, who, when they had all been seated, burnt perfume, and caused rose-water to be thrown over the visitors. He then stood up, with his arms extended, and pronounced a blessing over them.

My servant Sunday had for some time past been troubled with an attack of the spleen, and as I was without any medicine, he this evening requested me to allow a native woman to cup him, after the Bedouin fashion. To this I assented; and after gently rubbing the side, on the part affected, for upwards of an hour, she procured a sharp knife and scarified the skin over it; she then applied a horn, extracted the air contained within it by suction, and closed the aperture at the upper or smaller extremity with her finger. This was repeated several times with equal dexterity; and he afterwards found much relief from it.

I now directed all my efforts to the object of obtaining permission to depart; and it would be both tedious and unnecessary to state the various measures I was obliged to adopt in my several attempts to accomplish this. Suffice it, that after three days' hard fighting, and consenting to leave Mr. Cruttenden behind to explain matters to Sultan Abdallah, who was hourly expected, we were permitted to leave. An unpleasant incident also occurred at this time, which nearly marred all my arrangements, and produced serious consequences. An Arab, who had on more than one occasion behaved with some insolence on our former visit, continued now to thrust himself into our apartments, though repeatedly desired to leave them; until at length I was compelled to desire my servants to turn him out of the house; while I assured him myself, that if he ventured within again I would adopt other measures. A slight scuffle had thus ensued between him and the servants, but I had seen no more of him until this morning, when as I was seated on the terrace of the house reading I heard a scuffle in an adjoining house, and in a few minutes afterwards some women screamed violently; while I also observed several Arabs draw their swords and run towards the spot whence the noise proceeded. Conceiving that it was merely some disturbance among themselves, I was not at first inclined to pay much attention to it; but presently one of old Abdallah's daughters made her appearance below, and called out, that they were murdering my servant Sunday. I then immediately hastened to the spot, where I found, in place of this being the case, that Sunday had nearly murdered the Arab. I arrived just in time, for he was within an ace of being strangled. As it was no time for inquiries, I called Sunday off, and after desiring Abdallah to take charge of his opponent, walked again into the house. The Arabs appeared much excited, but contented themselves with flourishing their swords, shaking their spears, &c.; no one in my passage attempted either insult or injury. I left old Abdallah, without his turban, half mad with his endeavours to quiet them.

By Sunday's account (which I found afterwards correct), he was in a neighbouring garden, gathering some vegetables for our dinner, when the Arab came behind him unawares and struck him a tremendous blow with a club on the back of his head: but thanks to his Nubian birth for the thickness of his skull, and to his education among Englishmen for the use of his fists, this attack made little impression on him, and he returned it so briskly and effectually, that, had it not been for my arrival, his opponent would have had no reason to congratulate himself on his aggression. As I left the garden, the *qadi* (*cadhi*), who had been sent for, arrived, and in his presence a deposition regarding the case was taken. Numerous witnesses swore before him to the infliction and actual existence of numerous and horrible wounds - all of which, being mere scratches or bruises from several falls, had they permitted them to be washed, would have presented a very different appearance; so that presently, with this deposition, and accompanied by old Abdallah and one or two of the elders, he came up to me, representing the case in the light, that Sunday, a Christian slave, had ill-treated a *Muslim*. I thought matters had now gone far enough, and therefore represented to them that none serving under the English flag were slaves, but servants (a distinction, by the bye, not always understood in the East); and that so long as they served us faithfully we were bound to protect them: that, in turning the Arab out of the house, he had acted by my orders; and that, in short, for the future, I should, if any other attack was made on him, treat it as one addressed to myself, and act accordingly. This was treating the affair in the Arab fashion, for the *qadi* had no influence, and there were neither laws nor magistrates here. Unpromising as this affair looked at first - for they threatened to confine us still more closely to our houses and to stop our supplies - it eventually proved serviceable. On cool reflection they began to consider the consequences to themselves if they went too far; and as they knew the vindictive feelings of the Arab were rather increased than allayed, and that there was every reason to believe that I would perform my promise in case he should make any second attempt, they thought it better to get rid of me as soon as possible. In the evening, therefore, when sunset was announced, they all dispersed to their homes in order to concert measures for the morrow.

CHAPTER 5
DEPARTURE TO HACKABEE & SOUTHERN COAST

February 13. - Some camels were brought to me, in consequence, in the morning, which belonged to old Abdallah, who, willing to play the rogue on both sides, gave his neighbours to understand that I was to proceed at once to the ship; but, in truth, he struck a bargain with me for their hire for a month, with an understood, though not expressed permission, to use them on any part of the island which I pleased. The evening was far advanced, however, before all was arranged, and we were mounted and had left the town. I did not, therefore, proceed far beyond its precincts, but halted in a date-grove, about a mile and a half from the sea: where, even at this season, we found abundance of water, not only in running streams but in numerous wells. Many oxen and cows were collected under the shade of the trees, and the grass in some places was still luxuriant. After escaping from the myriads of flies and other vermin, the confined atmosphere of the town, and the pestering and importunity of its ignorant and bigoted inhabitants, the comfort of our tent, with the luxury of the pure air in the clear moonlight, which we now enjoyed, was an indescribable relief. It had been hinted to me from several quarters, that some violence was still contemplated towards us by the inhabitants of Hadibu, in return for the chastisement received by their townsman Ali; but if such a thing was ever thought of, they at least did not put it into practice; and we slept soundly until the following morning.

February 13. - At seven, we crossed the plain on our camels, in a S.E. direction, and at eight entered a narrow, steep valley, crossed by numerous streams, which led to the summit of the first range of hills from the sea. From this point we could discern the sea on both sides of the island very distinctly. The hills were composed of red feldspar, deposited in thick strata; the outer parts were much broken; and large fragments detached from them were strewn over the surface. The grass was scanty and withered, but there were a great many bushes. It rained violently the whole morning, and we and all our baggage got completely drenched. At nine o'clock we halted at a small date grove, about a mile to the left of the road, called Maasah Sadan, which has a stream of fresh water running through it. Here were some pearl millet fields and about half a dozen huts. The inhabitants were mongrel Arabs, who testified the utmost jealousy of all our movements; and when I produced my sketch-book they raised such a clamour that I was obliged to desist. My angles, bearings, and notes, on this and several subsequent days, were thus taken by stealth. Having partaken of a light meal and dried our clothes, we again resumed our journey to the south-eastward, across the island. This road must have been much frequented at some early period, for in several places there are traces of its having been built up, and the decayed and worn appearance of the material exhibits great age. From Maasah Sadan we passed along a valley in a direction S. E., in length seven miles, and breadth three. Between our track and the granite range, a lower chain extended, about 700 feet in height, which forms the S.W. side of the valley. That which forms the N.E. is lower.

Under the date-trees, as we passed along, I observed that there was a turf of fine grass; and even without them, the herbage was vigorous and healthy, and of a deeper tint than, judging from the stony nature of the ground, we should have expected to have met with. Some colocynths appear here, and also aloes; the hills are covered with bushes, but the plains are bare. The geological structure and formation of the hills are quite distinct from those on the western part of the island; a limestone hill never occurs here - they are all either feldspar or porphyry: in the former, though not so cavernous as the limestone, hollows are in like manner by no means uncommon.

At half-past two o'clock we crossed the extremity of a valley extending in a northerly direction towards the sea: in its centre a fine stream of pure clear water glides along; and on either side is a broad litre of date-trees. Our path now lay more to the eastward, and was crossed by numerous streams of fresh water. In this direction, the country, though considerably elevated above the level of the sea, is, with the exception of one high range, over which lies a road to Ras Moree, rather level and open. We passed some inhabitants, a few flocks of sheep, and several cows. Our route lay along one of the most considerable of the streams, with a date-grove on either side, until half-past four, when we halted at the foot of a pass, near a cascade and several pools of fresh water. Trees, with wide-spreading and luxuriant foliage, numerous aromatic plants, a fine clear cool atmosphere (therm. 69°), and a lovely moonlight night, rendered this one of the most delightful halting-places on the island. My tent was pitched on the smooth surface of the rock, a few yards from one of the most copious of these pools; and the murmuring of the stream over its pebbly bed was in unison with the sound of the distant cascade.

The first part of the evening was much enlivened by the presence of one of those itinerant traders who "vend their wares" among the mountains. They are in general a hardy, good humoured, and intelligent class; and wherever we fell in with them on the road, the chances were that they were singing some merry tune. Their occupation keeps them constantly moving about the island, and I have seen the Bedouins testify as much joy at the appearance of one of these men as if he had been one of their own relations returned from a long journey; a sheep is immediately killed, and every one does his best to entertain him. To the credit also of both parties be it said, that their bargains are, at least with the Bedouins, conducted in the same spirit. Nearly all the ghee which is shipped off from Hadibu is brought in by these men.

Dragon blood trees (Dracaena cinnabari) - Firmhin Plateau central Socotra

February 14. - This morning we ascended the pass, which was found too steep for us to ride up; the water gushed in all directions from the rock to the very summit; none, however, appearing on the opposite side, where the descent is less rapid. After crossing several streams and passing many herds of cattle, we halted at a small village called Amaro, consisting of about a dozen huts occupied by Arab herdsmen; fields of, pearl millet and date groves were here numerous. We pitched our tent in one of the latter, near a deep pool of running water; the hills continued of the same formation as those noticed yesterday; water was, however, far more plentiful, gushing in rills from the rocks in all directions; and several considerable streams, as will be seen by the map, intersected our track. There was, however, but little soil, and the bare rock showed itself frequently: but in its clefts and crevices many large trees have rooted themselves. Bushes were also numerous, and there was a great variety of parasitical plants. The borders of the streams appeared the only parts well adapted for cultivation, and on them, rice, vegetables, &c., might be grown to any extent; besides which, where running water exists, agriculturists would feel no difficulty in forming a soil.

After breakfast two females approached us with a present of milk and a young lamb: these ladies conversed freely with us unveiled, at which I was somewhat surprised, considering that they were married to Arabs, who evince or affect quite as much jealousy of their women as their brethren on the continent. When I mentioned this to young Suleiman, our guide (who was absent at the time, he cleared up the difficulty, by informing me, that their husbands were absent with their sheep, and had left their dames at home to make butter and spin wool; seeing the *Europeans* pass, they could not resist the temptation of conversing with us. The first thing which attracted their attention was my clothes, which were spread out in the sun to dry: they examined them most minutely, and laughed immoderately, as they discovered, or were told, the various purposes to which the different articles were applied: one expressed so much admiration of a pair of white trousers which she drew on in imitation of mine, that I could not but beg her acceptance of them. To her companion I was obliged to be equally liberal; and it would have disturbed the gravity of a more staid personage than myself, to have witnessed them strutting to and fro in their new habiliments before me. The pockets puzzled them a good deal, but by placing some needles and thread within them I soon explained their use. Both these females were Bedouins, and had fine features; but neither could be called handsome. There was, however, in their features, and in their fine dark eyes, an expression of much shrewdness and good-humour. "Twenty-six years of age," said one of them to me, "and not yet married?-why, who takes care of your house; prepares your meals, &c. &c.?" I endeavoured to explain this circumstance as well and as briefly as their voluble inquiries would allow me, but nothing would convince them that any benefit could compensate for so many years absence from connubial felicity, though, as a set-off against this, our custom of confining ourselves to a one wife was much commended. When they took leave I offered them my hand, they laughed, but gave theirs, when I assured them that it was our English custom. They promised, if I would remain another day, that they would come in the morning with a supply of milk, pearl millet, dates, and other Socotran luxuries, and would listen during the whole day to tales of the *Inglese* and their country; but to this, for obvious reasons, I could not now assent. It is singular that, in the course of this conversation, no allusion or inquiry was made as to whether or not I was a *Muslim*, usually the first question asked by all classes. but probably they thought that I was, and I did not wish to hazard my popularity by gratuitously undeceiving them. When the heat of the day was somewhat moderated, we again resumed our journey. Our route lay along a narrow valley, bounded on either hand by feldspar and porphyritic hills, about five hundred feet in height, with precipitous sides and table summits. The same stream by which we had made our halt led along the centre, and gradually increased both in width and depth, as we advanced; in some places it was four feet deep and thirty feet across, we should call such a stream a river, in Arabia; crossing and recrossing it by a bad road delayed us very much. My guide was also much alarmed for the feet of the camels; which not unfrequently, if kept wet, crack or ulcerate, and form sores, both difficult and tedious to cure. When we ascended the pass over Qalansiyah, two of our camels were laid up with bad feet, occasioned, our guide told us, by the heavy night dews which kept the grass wet even during the greater part of the day. I observed that the camels were, in general, very averse to taking the water, and when the stream was deep, they were not got over without some difficulty; yet when greatly tormented by the flies, they readily proceeded to a stream and rolled in it.

After riding for two hours we left this stream, the general direction of which was S. E., and struck off S. S. W., over a large hill. Primitive trap occurs here frequently, as do also fragments of pure and imperfect quartz. In about an hour we again met the stream, which had taken a turn round the eastern side of an elevated conical mountain, which our route now skirted on its western base; and at the approach of sunset we again halted on its banks. Scarcely any part of our road to-day was clear of date trees; small fields of pearl millet were also numerous, but no other traces of cultivation. The natives call the valley in which we encamped *Eshall*; here it is not more than 500 paces broad, and my guide told me that it grew narrower and was more thickly planted with date trees, as it approached the granite peaks. Several other valleys on this side take their rise near these barriers. At our halting-place the limestone again made its appearance, a long range of that formation, with its usual steep side and level summit, and about 700 feet in height, extending to the N.N.E., on the upper part of the ridge. I could discover numerous Dragon's Blood trees, and my guide assured me that some of the best gum on the island is gathered from this range; scattered *assett* and *eshaib* trees also line the sides, while numerous *Ziziphus spina-christi* and *bohain* trees extend along the base. Some Bedouins, who had seen our approach from the mountains, stole down towards our tent during the evening; whether they intended to make themselves discovered is uncertain, but at the moment one of their number approached rather close, I was engaged taking the meridian altitude of a star with the artificial horizon, and his surprise at seeing the quicksilver, the sextant, and my occupation, was so great, that an involuntary exclamation of astonishment escaped him. When he found that he was discovered, he at first attempted to make a retreat, but a few words from our guide reassured him, and he entered our tent - where his surprise, it will be anticipated, was not lessened by all he saw and witnessed.

February 15. - We followed the winding of the stream through a valley called Helofe, which at first had a very circuitous direction, but became afterwards nearly straight, in a north and south direction. On the one side the hills are of red feldspar, on the other of limestone, which in the exterior mass does not present the rounded form usual in the western portion, but is piled in huge blocks with straight fractures intersecting each other, so as to give the whole the appearance of gigantic masonry, as we advanced, the feldspar wholly disappeared, and we had the same continued succession of limestone as in the western part. When we halted to breakfast a Bedouin brought us a bowl of milk. he was a fine athletic young fellow, and as a specimen of his dexterity in climbing mountains, he, at our request, (after repeated assurances that he could effect it,) ascended a precipice so steep that in some places it was painful to the eye to follow him. It would be difficult to determine which serves them most on these occasions, their hands or their feet. Descending by the same dangerous and slippery track appealed far more difficult; but in a few minutes from his starting he was standing uninjured at the door of our tent. Towards noon we emerged from the mountain and entered on the low sandy belt which forms the southern coast of the island. The sea was now before us, but no ship was in sight. Concluding from the time which had elapsed since we last communicated with her that she must at least have passed this in her progress to Ras Moree, I turned my steps to the eastward and towards sunset halted near some huts, occupied by an old man and his family. The old man met us as we dismounted, and seeing that my servant was unwell, pressed us very much to enter his house, out of which he turned his wives, assuring us that it was quite at our service. When our tent was pitched, however, he saw its superiority over anything he could offer us, and then bitterly regretted his want of ability to serve us; but shortly afterwards he brought us a plentiful supply of milk, and, without my knowledge, killed a kid, and brought it to us most excellently cooked, after the native fashion, on some stones.

In the evening he told me that he possessed several flocks of sheep, which he had left on the hills under the guidance of the Bedouins; he himself residing here to procure fish, which he salts for his winter's store. For this purpose he employed no boat, but contented himself with collecting such fish as were entangled in the shallows, or left by the tide in the hollows of the rocks.

There were an amazing number of centipedes on this spot. We killed, while pitching the tent and during the evening, fourteen, not including young ones, and on the following morning we destroyed as many more. They were, however, small, and the natives said that the pain of their bite, though severe at first, does not last long. From hence to Ras Moree, by the way of the seashore, the road was described to me as being nearly impassable, as much from the want of water as from the rocky nature of the path. I was much disappointed at not being able to obtain from these people any intelligence of the ship, and began to fear that, during the late gales, she must have been blown off the island; at all events it seemed certain that she had not passed this, and it therefore became necessary for me to proceed alongshore to the westward in search of her. My only motive, at present, in wishing to communicate with her, was to inform the captain of Mr. Cruttenden being left behind in Hadibu.

DEPARTURE TO HACKABEE & SOUTHERN COAST

Meat cooking on stones

February 16. - In pursuance of this plan we now retraced our steps to the base of the mountains, along which the path wound; their height here varied from eight hundred to a thousand feet, and the whole range is table-topped - so that they appear to form an unbroken line for the whole distance that they are visible. Their direction is that of the sea- coast, and with the exception of a few capes or abutments projecting out, the line they follow is remarkably straight; the map will also show this. Not withstanding the hard and compact nature of the limestone which forms this chain, the action of the atmosphere has had its usual degrading effect; and has produced numerous hollows and caverns, besides a quantity of debris, everywhere observable along their base.

Near these hills are several *Hildebrandt's boxwood* bushes, and their sides and the valleys which break through them appeared to be also covered; but towards the sea-shore the belt is arid and sandy, and thickly covered, in some places, with the bushes and plants which are common to the desert plains of Arabia. Alongshore are almost continuous lines of sand-hills, of a pure sea-sand, which have been driven up by the south-west monsoon, and complete the dreary prospect. The only relief the eye meets with is from the lively green of the rock tree, which appears in many places to grow out of the sand, spreading its foliage over the hillocks, in low but close and thick masses. We passed a few goats and sheep browsing on the bare and withered herbs around; and halted during the heat of the day in the most eastern of some date-groves called Hackabee, which are planted on the sea-shore. Amidst the trees were a few wells, but the water was both brackish and bitter. None of our party, after being accustomed to the pure mountain-streams, could endure it. The trees are not more than a hundred yards from the beach, and I doubt if, to seaward, they can be seen over the sand-hills, - these have already attained a height equal to the trees, and as they appear to be rapidly increasing in size, they must, ere long, overwhelm the whole grove. Several of the outermost of the trees are already more than half buried, though this does not apparently affect either their growth or produce. It is asserted of these groves, that they bear two crops of fruit during the year, the one in May after the N. E., and the other in October after the S. W. monsoon; the produce 13 not, however, at either period held in equal estimation with that which is reared in other parts of the island. At this period the fruit was just forming. Contiguous to the grove are a few inclosures of cotton and tobacco.

An old woman surprised me to-day, sketching a hill by stealth; and raised a great clamour until I showed her the book and explained that it was for the purpose of amusing my harem, after which she was pacified. In the evening we pursued our way along the sandy belt, in which the feet of our camels sunk several inches at each step, making our progress slow and tedious. Dreary as this abode must be, especially in the S.W. monsoon, when it blows an almost continued tempest, several of the inhabitants reside on it; we passed several hamlets, and also a few detached houses. Nobody would, however, approach us, and we could learn as yet nothing respecting the ship, although we had come down twenty miles. At sunset we halted amidst some stunted bushes, a few yards from the sea. The night was cold in proportion to the heat of the day, and the ground was so filled with sand flies and red ants that it was almost impossible to sleep; we had also heavy showers of rain during the night. Fever had now seriously attacked Sunday, the only servant I had with me. I was myself far from well; one of the slaves was also laid up with fever, and the other was too unwell to be of any service: I had therefore, during the time we remained here, not only to attend to them, and prepare my solitary meal for myself, but also to assist with the camels. This and the few subsequent days, which I passed here waiting to get on board the ship, were the most unpleasant of my tour. I did not recover my health, nor did any of the party, until we breathed the pure air on the top of the hills about a week afterwards.

February 17. - Early this morning the ship was discovered beating up towards the point where we were encamped; but in the evening she anchored so far off shore that, notwithstanding all my signals, I found it impossible to attract attention. During the subsequent three days also the breeze continued with such violence from the eastward that I found it impracticable to communicate with her. Having at last therefore obtained a promise from a Bedouin that he would be on the look out, and would deliver a letter for the captain to the crew of the first boat which landed, I again retraced my steps to the groves at Hackabee, to conclude from thence the survey of the western part of the island. Our supplies of milk and sheep were procured from an old man who had been living in a sort of hermitage for the last fifty years. It was a cavern hollowed out of the rock, but differing in no ep and rugged, we lost our way several times, and were more than once near the precipice which sank to a tremendous depth on either hand. When we ched our halting-place, close to the bed of a stream, our slaves and the guide were npletely exhausted by the wet and cold, though the thermometer was not lower n 62° Fahrenheit, and a glass of brandy was necessary to restore them to their nted spirits. These men, unlike their masters, are by no means fastidious or rigid slims, and would swallow a gallon of spirits were it given them. A projecting k sheltered our tent from the full fury of the storm, at times it blew a perfect rricane; the thunder rolled over the lofty peaks above us, and shook the ground which we stood; huge masses of rock, and occasionally a tree torn from its roots, down the almost perpendicular sides of the mountain; the lightning flashed r the deeply-wooded ravines below us; while the rain, which fell in torrents, her fed than allayed the fury of the storm. The whole scene was magnificent and lime; but it had no charms for my associates, who, after hastily swallowing their ning meal, wrapped themselves up in all the clothes they could muster, and were n asleep.

February 23. - Our camels were found this morning to have taken advantage of ir master's fatigue and consequent neglect over-night, and having strayed up ong the mountains, could nowhere be seen. We were thus obliged, to halt for a while they were sought for; and I was the less displeased at the delay as we were bled by it thoroughly to dry our tent and baggage. A great many Bedouins and ne Arabs visited us, the former bringing us milk, and behaving with their ustomed kindness, while the latter were sullen, and told us in plain language that y wished us to move off. Whenever this proposal was made, and this was not frequently by the Arabs, I always adopted one plan, which was to laugh outright it. If, as on the present occasion when they observed the presents which we made the Bedouins, they afterwards wished to become familiar, I treated them with difference and neglect; and they then usually left, muttering some expression in Socotran language, which I neither could nor desired to understand. I was used this morning by observing the way our guide procured some milk before Bedouins came. He uttered a peculiar cry, and at the same time beat the anches of the trees with a stick; on hearing which the goats and sheep came mpering from all quarters to feed on the leaves which might fall from them, on ich the shepherds support them when the grass fails; and while so occupied they ade no resistance to being caught and milked.

February 24. - The Bedouins were most useful this morning in assisting us to ck up; and a few minutes after leaving, I saw about a hundred of them collected a small hamlet to see me pass. Continuing along the bed of the stream we passed o other hamlets. The trees along our route bore testimony to the fury of the cent tempest; the blasts, as they swept along the valleys, had wrenched many trees by the roots, and hurled them to some distance.

particular from those elsewhere described. I had the curiosity to go and visit him several times, and was always received with much attention and hospitality; he has one wife and two daughters, but they were kept carefully concealed from my view; the apartment to which they retired was another chamber communicating with the outer one by a small passage cut in the rock. I observed in one corner a large bundle of the inner shell of a turtle, and on inquiry found that a great number resort in the fine season to the southern shores of the island, for the purpose of depositing their eggs.

*Dragon's Blood (*Dracaena cinnabari*) & Camel Firmhin Plateau*

CHAPTER 6
TRAVEL TO RAS FELING

F*ebruary 19.* - We now returned towards the interior by a valley about a mile to the westward of that by which we came out some days before.

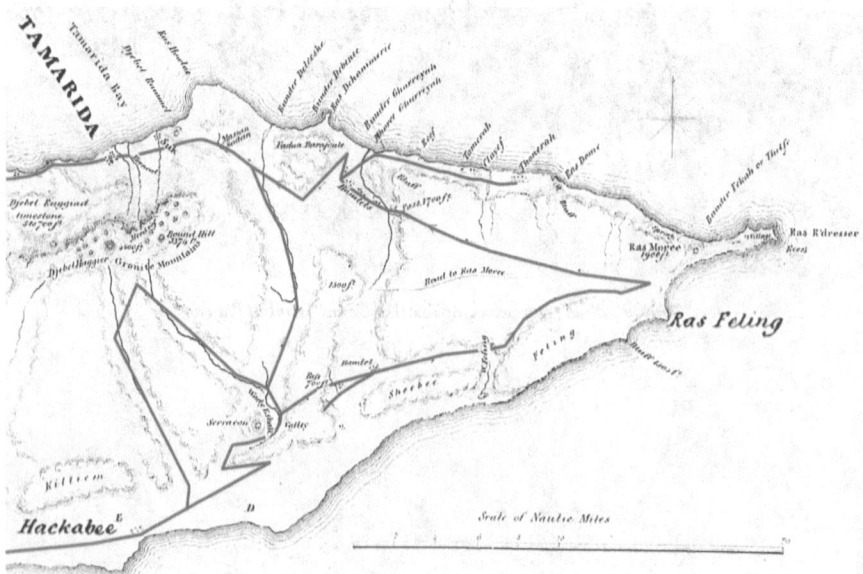

Easter Socotra

After passing the extremity of a stream which loses itself halted for a short time under a *bohain* tree, where the same strea broad and four deep. Some rushes grew here, about six feet in le at the extremity as pointed as a needle; the natives use them for n also for manufacturing ropes. This valley is altogether singular-lo is N.N.W., and it is about a mile and a half in breadth; the hills about 400 feet high; and their faces are nearly precipitous, with t appearance, and thickly clad with *camhane* and *assett* trees. The these caves as dwellings, and have their flocks on the intermedi while those who tend the date-groves in the valleys are Arabs. Du had a long conversation with one of the latter: he told me that h Mahrah tribe on the Arabian coast, who are fierce and turbulent of peace he disliked the continued broils which a residence amo and he had, in consequence, embarked with his wife, children, ar him, for this island, where his sole care and employment were som pearl millet fields, and sheep. One of his countrymen, who was time, expressed some surprise that I, who was an "unbeliever," sl and unarmed among Muslims and Arabs so bigoted as those of S to be. He suggested, indeed, that any individual, seated, as he wa seize me by the wrist or throat, so as to render me powerless, whil might plunder the baggage; but a sight of the pistols, which I alwa at my girdle, convinced him that I was anything but defencel attacks. All this passed, however, in the utmost good-humour, for same individual's house on the following morning, he brought ou milk which he pressed on my acceptance. At half-past two we a journey along the banks of the stream, in a N.N.W. direction u trees and pearl millet fields continued the whole distance. Towards at a spot where the valley opens out into a noble amphitheatre of peaks were before us, and the surrounding or nearest range could elevated than a thousand feet above us. I was so much pleased wit of water here, the purity and coolness of the atmosphere, and the of the scenery, that I pitched my tent under some *Ziziphus sp* determined to remain until my servant should return from the ship

February 20. - I passed this day in wandering with a Be mountains. Dragon's Blood trees and aloe plants were both ve entered several Bedouin huts, collected several specimens of flowers returned in the evening completely fatigued. A sound night's sl climate was my reward.

February 21 - We had slight rain during the greater part of cleaned up in the evening, and we moved up a steep pass to the nort returned with much fury, and my bed and baggage were compl Night also overtook us before we reached the summit; it "as very da

Adenium socotranum

I halted for a few minutes near another hamlet, each of the houses of which have one or two pearl millet enclosures attached to it; but they are miserable-looking hovels, and, to finish the picture, some goats were feeding on the grass which grew on their roofs. The soil was stony, but where the stones were removed it appeared productive. After leaving this, we in a few minutes entered Wady Eshall, and continuing along our former route, in an hour more we struck along another, running about N.N.E. This brought us close to Djebel Zafed; and in about an hour we halted in a valley, a few yards from a small village. A stream winds its way at the bottom of this valley, which is here very narrow, but afterwards spreads out and incloses some rounded hills, about seven hundred feet in height. Though the rock (limestone, with feldspar occurring occasionally) is but scantily covered with soil, yet it is clothed with abundance of grass; and the soil being in some places of greater depth than in others, in these a few large, though isolated, trees are seen springing forth. Under one of these we pitched our tent for the night; some cows, numerous flocks of sheep, and a more than usual quantity of pearl millet enclosures, rendered the scene rural and picturesque.

February 25. - My servant Sunday returned to-day from the ship: I was obliged to despatch him there for medical assistance. Captain Haynes, in his survey of the coast, had been much delayed by the late violent winds; and Sunday had been compelled to wait four days before a boat could land to take him off. When the Bedouins heard that I had received a supply of medicine, I had numerous applications for it: fevers and indigestion were the prevailing complaints.

February 26. - Leaving this spot, we passed for a short distance up the valley, ascending by a pass four hundred feet in height. From the top we obtained a splendid and magnificent view of the surrounding country. At 5 P.M., after passing several villages, we struck down a hill, leaving a pathway which leads to the Noged on our right, and after passing two more hamlets, now deserted, we halted on the summit of a small hill, a few yards from a third, consisting of fourteen houses. We had scarcely unpacked our camels when an old man, of the most venerable and patriarchal appearance, approached us, and inquired whether we should wish our supper to consist of mutton or grain, or both. He also brought us fire-wood (the hills here are bare of bushes and yield none), supplied us with milk, and in fact neglected nothing he thought would in any way add to our comfort. It was dark before we could get our tent pitched, but he and his friends assisted us greatly in doing so. I have the more pleasure in bearing testimony to the hospitality of this individual, since, among the Arabs of Socotra, he was the only one I can tax with such a dereliction from their Islamic creed as displaying good feeling towards a Christian.

February 27. - I rose early this morning and walked down, as was my usual custom, to bathe in the stream. The country I found of superior quality; the hills undulating and covered with the finest meadow-grass; with verdant fields of pearl millet in every hollow, and large flocks of sheep browsing above them; cows were particular from those elsewhere described. I had the curiosity to go and visit him several times, and was always received with much attention and hospitality; he has one wife and two daughters, but they were kept carefully concealed from my view; the apartment to which they retired was another chamber communicating with the outer one by a small passage cut in the rock. I observed in one corner a large bundle of the inner shell of a turtle, and on inquiry found that a great number resort in the fine season to the southern shores of the island, for the purpose of depositing their eggs.

*Dragon's Blood (*Dracaena cinnabari*) & Camel Firmhin Plateau*

CHAPTER 6
TRAVEL TO RAS FELING

February 19. - We now returned towards the interior by a valley about a mile to the westward of that by which we came out some days before.

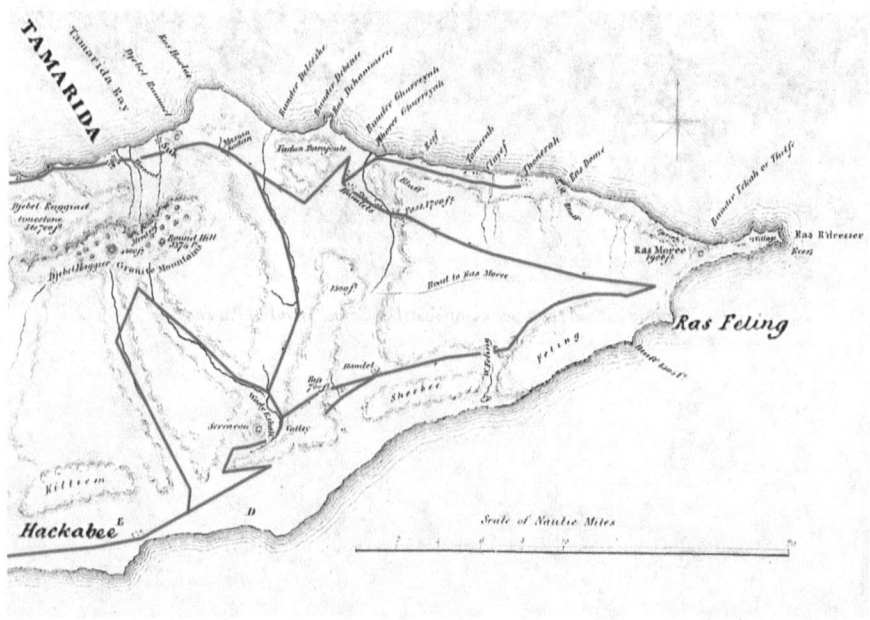

Easter Socotra

After passing the extremity of a stream which loses itself in the ground, we halted for a short time under a *bohain* tree, where the same stream was now ten feet broad and four deep. Some rushes grew here, about six feet in length, very stiff, and at the extremity as pointed as a needle; the natives use them for making baskets, and also for manufacturing ropes. This valley is altogether singular-looking; its direction is N.N.W., and it is about a mile and a half in breadth; the hills on either side are about 400 feet high; and their faces are nearly precipitous, with the usual cavernous appearance, and thickly clad with *camhane* and *assett* trees. The Bedouins. occupy these caves as dwellings, and have their flocks on the intermediate ranges of hills; while those who tend the date-groves in the valleys are Arabs. During our halt here I had a long conversation with one of the latter: he told me that he belonged to the Mahrah tribe on the Arabian coast, who are fierce and turbulent; but being a man of peace he disliked the continued broils which a residence among them entailed, and he had, in consequence, embarked with his wife, children, and all belonging to him, for this island, where his sole care and employment were some few date-groves, pearl millet fields, and sheep. One of his countrymen, who was with him at this time, expressed some surprise that I, who was an "unbeliever," should travel alone and unarmed among Muslims and Arabs so bigoted as those of Socotra are known to be. He suggested, indeed, that any individual, seated, as he was, near me, could seize me by the wrist or throat, so as to render me powerless, while his companions might plunder the baggage; but a sight of the pistols, which I always wore concealed at my girdle, convinced him that I was anything but defenceless against open attacks. All this passed, however, in the utmost good-humour, for when I passed the same individual's house on the following morning, he brought out a large bowl of milk which he pressed on my acceptance. At half-past two we again pursued out journey along the banks of the stream, in a N.N.W. direction up the valley; date trees and pearl millet fields continued the whole distance. Towards sunset we halted at a spot where the valley opens out into a noble amphitheatre of hills. The granite peaks were before us, and the surrounding or nearest range could in no part be less elevated than a thousand feet above us. I was so much pleased with the abundance of water here, the purity and coolness of the atmosphere, and the romantic beauty of the scenery, that I pitched my tent under some *Ziziphus spina-christi* trees, determined to remain until my servant should return from the ship.

February 20. - I passed this day in wandering with a Bedouin over the mountains. Dragon's Blood trees and aloe plants were both very numerous. I entered several Bedouin huts, collected several specimens of flowers and plants, and returned in the evening completely fatigued. A sound night's sleep in this fine climate was my reward.

February 21 - We had slight rain during the greater part of this day, but it cleaned up in the evening, and we moved up a steep pass to the northward. The rain returned with much fury, and my bed and baggage were completely drenched. Night also overtook us before we reached the summit; it "as very dark, the path was steep and rugged, we lost our way several times, and were more than once nearly over the precipice which sank to a tremendous depth on either hand. When we reached our halting-place, close to the bed of a stream, our slaves and the guide were completely exhausted by the wet and cold, though the thermometer was not lower than 62° Fahrenheit, and a glass of brandy was necessary to restore them to their wonted spirits. These men, unlike their masters, are by no means fastidious or rigid Muslims, and would swallow a gallon of spirits were it given them. A projecting lock sheltered our tent from the full fury of the storm, at times it blew a perfect hurricane; the thunder rolled over the lofty peaks above us, and shook the ground on which we stood; huge masses of rock, and occasionally a tree torn from its roots, slid down the almost perpendicular sides of the mountain; the lightning flashed over the deeply-wooded ravines below us; while the rain, which fell in torrents, rather fed than allayed the fury of the storm. The whole scene was magnificent and sublime; but it had no charms for my associates, who, after hastily swallowing their evening meal, wrapped themselves up in all the clothes they could muster, and were soon asleep.

February 23. - Our camels were found this morning to have taken advantage of their master's fatigue and consequent neglect over-night, and having strayed up among the mountains, could nowhere be seen. We were thus obliged, to halt for a day while they were sought for; and I was the less displeased at the delay as we were enabled by it thoroughly to dry our tent and baggage. A great many Bedouins and some Arabs visited us, the former bringing us milk, and behaving with their accustomed kindness, while the latter were sullen, and told us in plain language that they wished us to move off. Whenever this proposal was made, and this was not unfrequently by the Arabs, I always adopted one plan, which was to laugh outright at it. If, as on the present occasion when they observed the presents which we made to the Bedouins, they afterwards wished to become familiar, I treated them with indifference and neglect; and they then usually left, muttering some expression in the Socotran language, which I neither could nor desired to understand. I was amused this morning by observing the way our guide procured some milk before the Bedouins came. He uttered a peculiar cry, and at the same time beat the branches of the trees with a stick; on hearing which the goats and sheep came scampering from all quarters to feed on the leaves which might fall from them, on which the shepherds support them when the grass fails; and while so occupied they made no resistance to being caught and milked.

February 24. - The Bedouins were most useful this morning in assisting us to pack up; and a few minutes after leaving, I saw about a hundred of them collected at a small hamlet to see me pass. Continuing along the bed of the stream we passed two other hamlets. The trees along our route bore testimony to the fury of the recent tempest; the blasts, as they swept along the valleys, had wrenched many trees up by the roots, and hurled them to some distance.

also numerous. In one spot close to the stream I observed a large field of beans growing; but some females who were plucking them fled with much precipitation as I approached. At half-past nine we proceeded to the eastward. The valley we entered was broad at the entrance, but became narrow as we advanced, until after an hour and a half, when we found the extremity blocked up by an immense mountainous wall, which threw a natural barrier across it. Close to this point we therefore ascended a pass, about four hundred feet in height; we proceeded on foot, the ascent being very steep and slippery for the camels. From the upper part we continued along a level plain, occasionally passing sheep and oxen; we then entered another valley, where were a great many date-trees, and a large village contiguous to them, on a hill. Close to this is another pass, about four hundred feet in height; whence the limestone hills continue at nearly the same level to Ras Moree. There is no difference between the appearance of these hills and those already described at the western end of the island. At half-past eleven we halted, for a few minutes, near another village, occupied by Bedouins; the females came round us and were more than usually importunate; they were obliged, however, to content themselves with a few needles and thread. There are no wells here, and when the water supplied by the natural reservoirs is exhausted, the inhabitants repair, with their flocks, to the streams below.

The country, as we advanced in the direction of Ras Moree, became more flat and uninteresting. Neither granite nor feldspar occur here; but some huge fragments of limestone, ten or fifteen feet high, with sharp and rugged points, and level bases, were founding on the plains; narrow, precipitous ravines, resembling fissures, also occurred frequently, their extremities being blocked up suddenly, as by a dead wall. In one of these plains we passed a rude stone seat, in which the Bedouins seat their boys when they circumcise them; a short distance from this were two burying-grounds; and in the centre between these, a ruinous building which, my guide said, was an ancient chapel. About an hour after sunset we halted close to the verge of a precipice, about two miles north of Ras Feling.

February 28. - I now determined to remain here a day, in hopes of the ship making her appearance. We were encamped at the termination of the elevated land which here sinks precipitously, and leaves a low tongue of land, extending from the base of the hills and forming the eastern extremity of the island, called, by the Arabs, Ras Moree: it is sandy and barren. A few ruins are found on it, but the natives have no legend respecting them. Our height, where encamped, was 1700 feet above the level of the sea; but the view was not by any means so beautiful or striking as that over Qalansiyah; a limestone hill, rising 900 feet above us, and narrow as a wall, being the only remarkable object. Large sheets, or laminae, have been splintered from this, and precipitated down the precipice; and others appear in a very precarious situation.

CHAPTER 7
RETURN TO PALINURUS

March 1. - The ship not appearing, we left our place of encampment shortly after noon, to return to Hadibu by the direct road, which is to the northward of that by which I came up to the cape. The country is here poor and barren, but Dragon's Blood trees are numerous. At half-past one o'clock we passed a valley, running north and south, in which are some wells of water, the first we have seen on the elevated land. From hence the country gradually improves; the grass is thick and fine, and the soil, which is dark and rich, appears well adapted for cultivation. *Bohain* and *tuk* trees are numerous; and the birds, which were sheltered from the heat of the sun's rays amidst their branches, carolled gaily with a not unpleasing note. A continuous line of cavernous habitations skirted the road during the greater part of our day's journey. Cows, with sheep and goats, were numerous. The atmosphere was clear and exhilarating, and everything had a gay and picturesque appearance. In the evening I was agreeably surprised by the appearance of Mr. Cruttenden, who, finding that some unforeseen event had prevented Abdallah's arrival, had determined on joining me directly the Arabs would allow him to leave the town. He was enabled to effect this, at length, through the assistance of some Mahrah Arabs, who brought him a camel after dark, on which he mounted, and, travelling all night, was the next morning beyond pursuit. We halted, when we met him, near a deep reservoir of water, the adjoining scenery to which is very remarkable. The whole of the hills around swarm with inhabitants, and when we made our appearance they came crawling out of their caves like ants from an ant-hill. The grass *Pennisetum dichotomum* is very plentiful here, and was so annoying that to avoid it I pitched my tent among the rocks. I had thus a full view of this community: some noble-looking cows were feeding around. This part of the island is the most picturesque and promising that I have seen.

Delisha Beach

March 2. - At seven this morning we resumed our journey, passing over a very similar country to that described yesterday. After two hours' riding we descended a pass, and found at its base a stream of fresh water, many cows, and much of the surrounding country thickly wooded. With the exception of the *eshaib* being more, and the *Ziziphus spina-christi* and *tuk* trees less numerous, the vegetation was the same as yesterday. At half-past nine we descended another pass, which in magnificence and romantic grandeur may be thought to exceed any other part of the island. It was a narrow ravine, at least 1400 feet deep; the southern side descending in a bare perpendicular wall of reddish-coloured lime- stone, the northern side almost equally steep, and both these and the bottom thickly wooded.

Di Hamri coral reefs

Down the centre a large stream takes its course, leaping from rock to rock, and forming sparkling and elegant cascades. Two of these, where the stream is from ten to fourteen feet wide, have a fall of forty feet, and are received in capacious basins hollowed in the lock, within which the water looks clear, blue, and deep. Our road lay along the northern bank, and new scenes of beauty were discovered at every turn which its winding course compelled us to take. We halted at the foot of the pass, close to a date-grove, where we breakfasted. The rock here is a similar limestone to that above described; but a curious effect is occasionally produced by narrow spires of feldspar rising up through it to the height of three or four hundred feet. At half-past two in the afternoon we again proceeded; the mountains forming a complete amphitheatre round us, no side being apparently open. The direction of our route was about W.N.W., leading across many shallow valleys and low hills, extending like ribs from a hill to the right. We passed the extremity of this at 4 P.M.; four miles to the southward of the pass we thus descended, there is another road, connected with the one by which I first crossed the island, which also leads to Ras Moree. By both the ascent is about 1900 feet. At sunset we halted under a large tamarind-tree, about a mile from the sea, and near a large inlet, called Khoree Curreyah, or Ghurreyah, the entrance of which is nearly blocked up by sand, though still admitting small boats. On our way to this halting-place we passed no fewer than seven hamlets, each containing from seven to fifteen houses, so that along both roads the country is thickly peopled. The inhabitants here are called Lahsee, and are about 150 in number. They are Bedouins, and do not allow (in which they are singular) the Arabs to intermarry with them. Many of the date-trees here are very old, but they appear to bear fruit as long as they stand; some of them are so far decayed near the root, that they would not measure more than seven or eight inches in diameter.

March 3. - After the cool air on the hills, we found this last night intolerably warm, and left at six, winding our way round a hill called Fadan Derafonte, which sounds very like Portuguese. It abounds Dragon's Blood trees and aloes; the greatest height of any of its points is 1000 feet. This and several other hills in the neighbourhood exhibit a somewhat different structure from the others, having an upper stratum of light-coloured limestone super-posed on the general mass of the hill. At half-past eight o'clock we came on our former road, leading to the Noged, and after crossing the ridge of hills and entering on Hadibu plain, which we crossed in a N. N. E. direction, we entered a valley up which lies the road over the granite mountains. Continuing to ascend this by a path along the edge of the ravine, we found the road as we advanced become very steep; and our progress was continually interrupted by large blocks or fragments of rocks, over which it was necessary to scramble, and which, after the camels had had several severe falls, at last compelled us to halt.

March 4. – Shortly after sunrise, we set off on foot to finish the remainder of our ascent. Notwithstanding the steepness and ruggedness of the path, it is used occasionally by the Bedouins, while proceeding with their bullocks across the island. After three hours' severe exertion, we reached the base of the granite spires, which rose from 800 to 1000 feet above us. After taking off our shoes, and proceeding for a short distance along a cleft pointed out to us by our guide as a path by which the mountaineers occasionally proceeded to the summit, we found it would be impracticable to proceed without imminent risk of slipping down the precipice, and there was no object of importance to be gained by our attaining it. I thought it advisable, therefore, to return with our guides to some orange-trees, where we found Bedouins waiting with milk to receive us. From the exertions we had used in ascending thus far (4400 feet) we were bathed in perspiration; and, as we had not taken the precaution to provide ourselves with warm clothing, we suffered much from the great keenness of the wind and atmosphere while endeavouring to light a fire by which we could dry our clothes. I could not but remark a property in the atmosphere here which I have not before heard of, though I imagine it must exist in other elevated districts: our guide, who had been daily in the habit of lighting our fire In the plains below by means of rubbing together two pieces of wood, found it impracticable here until after repeated attempts and great exertion.

The copious dews which descend at night, and the frequent and heavy showers which occur at all periods, together with the decreased temperature, combine to bring about various differences between the aspect of the country here and the plain below. The soil is here darker and richer, the grass higher and more luxuriant, thickly-wooded spots are inter mingled with rounded grassy hillocks, and numerous rills and streams gush forth between and across them. During our ascent, we passed several of these which might be heard and not seen, and others which were running in a clear and sparkling stream over the bare rock.

Our visit to these mountains, among which we remained two days, furnished us with information on a point of some importance in reference, at least, to our probable future occupation of the island. Judging from the great height of the average range of the thermometer in the S.W. monsoon, band the assertion of the inhabitants as to the insalubrious effects on the constitutions of visitors of the N. E. monsoon, it may appear questionable if our troops or agents, without a great sacrifice to health, could remain at Hadibu. But the height of these mountains, with any temperature below, would ensure a cool and salubrious atmosphere; while the nature of their soil, and the abundance of water found among them, remove any other objection which could be urged against a permanent residence on the island.

March 6. - Descending the mountains, I remained a day at the village of Suq, seeking in vain for some further traces of the Portuguese, or any other remains. While strolling along the seaside shortly afternoon for this purpose, the day being intensely hot, I observed something at a distance which a man had just quitted, who, however, seeing me direct my steps towards it, halted until I came up, and returned with me to the spot. Here I found that a hollow had been made in the loose sand of which the beach was composed, and in this, lying on his back, and protected only from the fierce and scorching heat of the sun's rays by a tattered piece of cloth, was an old man apparently in the last stage of existence; he was unable to speak, but before him were placed a few fragments of half-broiled fish and some pearl millet , of which he had lightly partaken. On inquiring of my companion the meaning of what I saw, he told me with much nonchalance, that when a man or woman become too old to work, it is their custom to place them in the earth in this manner; food being brought them daily until they expire, when a little earth thrown over them completes their already more than half-formed grave. And although during my stay on the island I had not before met an instance of this kind, I have been assured by the inhabitants of Hadibu that it is of not unfrequent occurrence.

March 7. - This morning we again entered Hadibu; whence we shortly afterwards re-embarked in our ship. I conclude this narrative, then, with a brief abstract of the information regarding the Island of Socotra, which the journey detailed in it enabled me to collect.

CHAPTER 8
BACKGROUND TO SOCOTRA

Form and Geographical Features of the Island. -The Island of Socotra ls of the shape of an acute spherical triangle, having for its vertex the flat promontory towards the east called Ras Moree, and presenting its convex side to the southward, as it were a bulwark against the swell of the ocean whose waters are rolled against it. Here, too, the coast preserves nearly an unbroken line; but on the northern side it is broken into a succession of small bays; and the base is also similarly indented. The whole island may be described as a pile of mountains, of nearly equal height, almost surrounded by a low plain, extending from their base to the margin of the sea. This is of irregular width, varying from two to four miles, excepting near Ras Feling and Has Shuab, where the mountains rise up perpendicularly from the sea, and it disappears altogether. Throughout the whole extent of this belt, with the exception of those parts which are watered by the mountain streams in their progress towards the sea, and some' spaces hereafter specified, the soil is hard, and does not in its present state appear to any considerable degree susceptible of cultivation. The southern side, though considerably less fertile than the northern, is yet, in the vicinity of Ras Moree, reasonably productive; but to the westward it is as arid and barren as the worst parts of Arabia. There the force of the south-west wind has blown the sand up from the sea-shore, where it is so fine as to be nearly impalpable; and formed it into a continuous range of sandhills, which extend parallel to the beach for several miles, whence it spreads over the plain, and is even in some places deposited in great quantities at a distance of three miles from the sea, at the base of the mountains, which there form a barrier, and alone prevent it from overwhelming the natural soil of the whole island. On the northern side the plain is stony, and covered with a dwarfish bush (the *Hildebrandt's boxwood*) about six feet in height, the foliage of which appears to be retained during the north- east season of the year, and gives to the space where it grows the appearance, from a distance, of being clothed with verdure. Such is the appearance and nature of the sea-coast, but the high land exhibits a great variety of soil and surface. As a general remark, it may however be observed, that nothing in the north-east monsoon presents a stronger contrast than the eastern and western sides of the island. While the former is destitute of verdure, has scanty pasturage, and, with the exception of some places near the sea, has no other water than what is retained in natural reservoirs, the latter is supplied with frequent streams, its valleys and plains afford luxuriant grass, herds of cattle are numerous, and the scenery in many places is equal to that of our own country.

Beginning with the granite range of mountains in the vicinity of Hadibu, as the most central and lofty, steep valleys may be first stated as dividing it into narrow ridges, which extend in a north-east and south-westerly direction. Of these, the upper range is composed of coarse, grey granite, which protrudes its spires to the height, as was ascertained by measurement, of five thousand feet. Their summits are consequently seldom free from clouds; but when the weather is clear, their appearance is broken and picturesque. The lower part of this chain is covered with the same dwarfish tree as the plains higher up, with a considerable variety of other trees and aromatic plants; but the granite spires merely nourish a light-coloured moss, and are destitute of verdure. Connected with the granite range, and extending from north to south, a lower range is found, averaging in height about 1900 feet, and composed of a compact cream-coloured primitive limestone. From this the hills diverge in short ranges to the sea-shore, their outline being mostly smooth, with table summits and rounded sides, except those nearest the sea, which mostly present a steep wall. The whole of the hills in the western part of the island are similar in their appearance, elevation, and construction to this range.

As the whole Island of Socotra may be considered one mass of primitive rock, we cannot expect to find it distinguished by any remarkable fertility of soil; I yet found it so varied that it is difficult to speak of it in general terms. The summit and sides of the greater part of the mountains composing the eastern part of the island present the smooth surface of the rock entirely denuded of soil, though in some places the rain has worn hollows and other irregularities, in which is lodged a shallow deposit of light earth, and a few shrubs spring forth. On the summits of the hills on the northern side of the island, and against the sides and elevated regions in the vicinity of the granite peaks, a dark rich vegetable mould is found, which nourishes a thick and luxuriant vegetation. In the plain about Hadibu, and some portions near Qadub, are several beautiful valleys, such as that I crossed on my return from Ras Moree. The soil is a reddish-coloured earth, which nourishes, at certain seasons, an abundant supply of grass, and appears well adapted for the cultivation of grain, fruit, and vegetables. In the valleys through which the streams flow, not only are there extensive groves of date-trees, but the existence of a broad border of beautiful turf, occasional inclosures of pearl millet , and, though but rarely, a plantation of indigo or cotton, indicate no want of fertility in the soil. The natives themselves, indeed, are aware of this, and speak of their own stupidity and indolence as the work of fate.

Climate - Though Socotra is situate only a short distance from the continents of Africa and Arabia, and is in fact in the same parallel with their most parched and burning plains, yet, from both monsoons blowing over a vast expanse of water, it enjoys, at least as compared with them, a remarkably temperate and cool climate. A register of the thermometer, kept in the north-east monsoon, from the 12th of January to the 13th of March, exhibits during that time the mean daily temperature of 70 ½ °, while several streams, at but a short distance from the level of the sea, indicated the mean annual temperature at 74 ¼ ° (Fahr.). On the hills it is still cooler; and the great elevation of the granite mountains would enable settlers to choose their own climate. Until a few days before we quitted the island the monsoon blew very fresh, and at times the wind swept through the valleys with a violence which I have rarely seen equalled. The sky was usually overcast, and while in the countries of Asia and Africa, under the same parallel, some time was yet to elapse before the termination of the dry season, Socotra enjoyed frequent and copious rains, due to her granite mountains, the lofty peaks of which obstruct the clouds, causing them to deposit their aqueous particles, to feed the mountain streams, or precipitate themselves in plentiful showers over the surrounding country.

On our second visit, in the south-west monsoon, during the time the vessel remained in Hadibu Bay, we found the average, as will be seen by the Meteorological Table appended, much higher than the above; but it should not at the same time be forgotten that we were then under the high land on the lee side of the island, and the wind became heated in its passage across it. On the windward side of the island, the summits of the mountains, and the open part of the coast between Ras Moree and Hadibu Bay, the weather was at this time also delightfully cool.

But though our register was thus affected by local causes, and can be considered as only a partial account of the temperature and state of the atmosphere on the island generally, yet, as a register of the effects of the monsoon at the principal port, it is very valuable. It will be seen, that in place of the dark cloudy weather with which this season commences in India, it was here for the most part clear and cloudless; and that the stars at night shone forth with uncommon brilliancy. During this period, also, when it was blowing nearly a hurricane, and when the gusts swept down from the mountains with a force almost irresistible, throwing up the water in sheets, and keeping our decks, and masts to the height of the tops, continually wet with the spray, we had with the exception of a dense white canopy of clouds formed, like the table-cloth over the Table Mountain at the Cape, before the setting in of the breeze with its utmost degree of violence, the same clear and cloudless weather. The wind, when it blew strongest, felt dry; and indeed, such was its siccity, that water dropped on the deck dried up instantaneously. As Is usual with winds of this nature, we felt hot or cold according to the previous state of our own skins. If we were perspiring, we felt cool; but otherwise, we felt hot, feverish, and uncomfortable. And, notwithstanding the heat of the wind at Hadibu at this season, the natives do not ascribe to it any ill effects; it would merely appear from their testimony, that intermittent fevers are prevalent at the change of either monsoon, and few of the Arabs from the coast, who reside here any time, escape them.

Natural Productions. --Among the few natural productions of importance which are found in Socotra, the first rank is due to the *Aloe spicala* or *Socotrina*, called, in the language of the island, *tayef,* and by the Arabs, *soobah*. For this plant the island has been famous from the earliest period, and it is too well known to need description here. It is found growing spontaneously on the sides and summits of the limestone mountains, at an elevation of from five hundred to three thousand feet above the level of the plains. The plants appear to thrive only in parched and barren places, its leaves are plucked at any period, and after being placed in a skin the juice is suffered to exude from them. In this state they are brought into Hadibu and Qalansiyah, whence they are mostly shipped for Muscat, where their price varies very considerably. In 1833 the best sold for one rupee the Bengal seer (nearly an English pound); while, of the more indifferent, four seers might be procured for a dollar. The Socotrine aloes, when pure. are the finest in the world; but, owing to the careless manner in which they are gathered and packed, they contract many impurities, and their value becomes proportionally deteriorated. Formerly every part of the island produced the aloe, and the whole was fanned out to different individuals, the produce being monopolized at a fixed price by the Sultan. The boundaries, however, thus set up, which consisted of loose stone walls, and were carried with immense labour over hill and dale, though they still remain, under the present unsettled government no longer distinguish property. The descendants of the owners to whom the several fields were formerly allotted, have either withdrawn their claims, or these are forgotten. At present, any one collects the aloe leaves who chooses to take the trouble, and nothing is levied on account of the Sultan. As they lodge but little in warehouses, and merely collect when the arrival of a ship or *Baghla* creates a demand, the quantity purchased or produced has been supposed to be much less than it is in reality, but on the west side of the island the hills, for an extent of miles, are so thickly covered with the plants, that it is not likely, at any future period, that the whole quantity will be collected which might be procured. The quantity exported within the last five years has varied very much; in 1883, it amounted to eighty-three skins, or two tons.

Next in importance to the aloe comes the Dragon's Blood tree (*Pterocarpus draco* – today *Dracaena cinnabari*), the gum from which (*Sanguis draconis*) is also collected by the Bedouins, at all seasons. As this gum is known to be produced by several trees, and the species in which it is found in Socotra may not therefore be known in Europe, I shall give a short account of it. Like the aloe, it is usually met with on the hills, rarely at a less elevation than eight hundred, and frequently as much as two thousand feet, above the level of the sea. The trunk, at the height of six feet from the ground, varies from twelve to eighteen inches in diameter; and its height is from ten to twenty feet. The branches are numerous, but short, and thickly intertwined with each other. The leaves are of a coriaceous texture, about twelve inches in length, sword-shaped, and pointed at the extremity; at the base, where they are sessile, they are somewhat extended, and resemble the leaves of the pine-apple. At this part they are connected with the branch of the tree, and extending from it in an indefinite number, they assume a fan-like shape; several of these together form the upper part of the tree, and their variety in shape and distribution gives rise to most fantastic appearances. We were not sufficiently fortunate to obtain any specimens of the flowers, but botanists describe it as belonging to the seventeenth class of Linnaeus, and to the natural order *Leguminosae*.

The gum exudes spontaneously from the tree, and it does not appeal usual on any occasion to make incisions in order to procure it. Two kinds were shown me; one, of a dark crimson colour, called *moselle*, is esteemed the best; and its price at Muscat is from six to eight rupees the Bengal seer. Dragon's Blood is called by the Arabs, *dum khoheil*; and *edah*, by the Socotrans. I was frequently assured, that not one-tenth of the quantity which might be procured was ever collected by the Bedouins; as with the aloes, this appears to be consequent on there being no regular demand. From a tree called, in the language of the island *amara*, a light-coloured» gum is also procured, which is slightly odoriferous, but inferior to that called *aliban*, on the Arabian coast. Sketches and descriptions were taken of the other varieties of trees on the island, but as they are not suitable for building or any useful purpose, and are merely remarkable for being indigenous to the island, it does not seem necessary to swell this paper with more than a few general remarks respecting them.

The most singular among them are two varieties which are called, in the language of the island, *assett* and *camhane*; both grow in very rocky places, and derive nourishment from the soil lodged in cells and cavities. The whole diameter of their trunks consists of a soft, whitish cellular substance, so easily cut through that we could divide the largest of them with a common knife. Camels and sheep feed all the leaves of the *camhane*, but reject those of the *assett*. A milk-white juice exudes from the trunk and leaves of both, the nature of which Is so acrid, that if it penetrates to the eyes the pain is almost intolerable. Several stems branch forth from the same family of roots, and the *assett*-trees mostly divide, at a short distance from the ground, into several branches. From the relative proportion between their height and diameter, and the few leaves of foliage borne by them compared to their bulk, the most singular and grotesque appearances are often produced; some are not more than five feet in height, while their base covers a greater extent in diameter. Both varieties, during the north-east monsoon, bear a beautiful red flower. Since leaving Socotra, I have met the same trees in the vicinity of Mukalla (Maculla), but I can find no mention made of them in any work within my reach.

The *eshaib*-tree is remarkable as resembling, in its light and graceful form, the weeping-ash of England. Notwithstanding the slender dimensions of its trunk, and its being always slightly inclined in a direction contrary to the prevailing south-westerly breezes, it appears to be capable of withstanding the full force of a tropical storm. From the great length of the petiole, the leaves hang loose, and are easily shaken by the wind, presenting an appearance similar to that produced by the "light quivering aspen.' A more beautiful or tasteful mourner over an urn or tomb than this plant could not be selected.

One of the largest trees on the island is the *Socotran Pomegranate*, which produces a species of wild grape, bearing however but little resemblance to that fruit, unless in its clustering form and rounded shape. The distribution of the branches of this and all the other large trees (excepting the *eshaib*) is fantastic, tortuous, and knotty. The *bohain-* tree is scarcely inferior in size to the *Socotran Pomegranate*. It has a broad leaf resembling the English sycamore, of which the camels and sheep are very fond. The tamarind, or *tamurthudy*, Indian date, as it is styled by the Arabs, and the *tuk*, a species of wild fig, are very frequently found amidst the mountains. From the fruit of the former (the tamarind) the natives obtain a cooling and refreshing drink; and the umbrageous foliage of the latter offers, during the heat of the day, to the Bedouins a most grateful shade: they frequently remain encamped for several days under these trees. On the sea-shore there is a small tree, the inner bark of which the natives eat, and pronounce to be very good. The wood of a tree named *Hildebrandt's boxwood* or *malarah*, which abounds in every part of the island, is so hard that our seamen used it for the same purposes as *lignum vita*: is applied to, such as sheaves for blocks, splicing fids, &c. If I add to these the date and the *brah*, all the principal trees will have been enumerated which came under my observation. The foliage of the date-tree here, as in India, is more scanty than in Arabia or Persia. A large collection of plants was obtained; but the botanist, on the summit of the granite mountains, would yet meet with a rich harvest. From the granite spires, and also on some of the highest of the limestone hills, the Bedouins collect a grey-coloured moss, called *sheenah*, which is used by the Arab females to dye their faces of a yellow colour. It adheres firmly to the rock, the whole surface of which is covered with it. As agriculture is almost wholly unknown on the Island of Socotra, the only grain cultivated on any part of the island is a species of millet, called pearl millet ; this is preferred to any other because it requires little attendance, and will produce a crop at any season. Provided there is water in its vicinity, little solicitude is shown about the quality of the soil selected for its culture; merely the loose stones are removed, and with them a wall is built, to prevent the inroads of the cattle. The soil within is somewhat loosened with a pointed stick, for they have no implement of husbandry; and after being divided by embankments into small squares, the crop remains until it is ripened and fit to cut down. When milk is abundant, and they can obtain dates, pearl millet is rarely partaken of; but when the supply of these is uncertain, or scanty, it forms the chief article of their food. It adds not a little to the value which they place on this grain, that they are enabled to keep it uninjured for a long period. No pearl millet is grown on the western side of the island; but on the eastern, the enclosures amidst the valleys are very numerous. It is, however, to their date groves, next to their flocks, that the inhabitants look for their principal means of support; though, with the exception of a small one at Qalansiyah, and another on the west side of the granite peaks, these are also confined to the eastern portion of the island. Here the borders of the numerous streams are lined for miles with them; some being fecundated at the latter end of December, and others as late as the early part of March; by which means they secure to themselves a supply of fresh dates for two months. Those parts of the island which are warmest produce the first crop.

Notwithstanding the large quantities collected from the whole of these groves, the native supply is insufficient for the consumption of the inhabitants, and a large import takes place annually from Muscat. In the vicinity of Hadibu are some inclosures of beans; and a little tobacco is grown, sufficient {or the consumption of the inhabitants. On the granite mountains some wild orange-trees are found, producing a sour and bitter fruit; and a species of wild yam grows in the same regions; but no other fruits or vegetables of any description, so far as known. I have already noticed the fertility of the soil in some places inland, and the extraordinary advantages it possesses in its numerous streams; but both are utterly disregarded by the natives. The whole of the land in the vicinity of the granite peaks is, in the highest degree, susceptible of cultivation, and grain, fruit, or vegetables, to any extent, might be reared in the plains near Hadibu, and amidst the rich valleys in the direction of Ras Moree. The face of the hills on the northern side might be tilled and cultivated in the same manner as is customary in Syria and Palestine. In a word, were it not for the prevailing ignorance and sloth among its inhabitants, Socotra, in a few seasons, might be rendered as celebrated for the extent and variety of its productions, as it is now perhaps remarkable for their small number and little comparative value.

Natural History. - The only animals we saw in Socotra were camels, sheep, asses, oxen, goats, and civet cats. The camels are as large as those of Syria, but are more remarkable for strength than speed. Continually ascending and descending the mountain passes by bad roads, they become nearly as sure-footed as mules; but, being constantly fed on succulent bushes and herbs, they do not, if this food is taken from them, display the same endurance of thirst as those of Arabia. When confined to the parched shrubs which grow on the low land, they require to be watered daily. Camels are principally used by the traders while seeking ghee, &c. among the mountains, and by the inhabitants when transporting dates or firewood to, and from, the interior. The whole number on the island does not exceed two hundred. For those I took with me I paid severally six dollars per month. The price for which they are sold is usually from twenty to thirty dollars. Cows are very numerous near Hadibu and on the mountains in its vicinity. They are usually of the same colour as that which distinguishes the Alderney breed in England, but their size does not exceed that of the small black Welsh cattle. The hump, which marks those of India and Arabia, is not observed hem; and they have the dewlap, which is supposed to be a distinguishing feature in the European cow. The pasturage for them is abundant; and their appearance is consequently sleek and fat; their flesh, when young, is of the most superior quality. The natives keep them mostly for the sake of their milk, with which the ghee, so much in estimation in Arabia and Africa, is made. They are not, therefore, solicitous to part with them, and the prices which they demand for those in condition is proportionately high; ten dollars were paid for those we purchased. Their flesh was pronounced equal to that of our finest English oxen. We had reason to believe also that bullocks or cows are rarely killed by the people of Socotra, excepting at either the death of some individual possessing a herd of them, or some influential personage; indeed, so anxious do they appear on these occasions to prevent the possibility of this ceremony being omitted, that I have known them, when any of their family was sick, send for five or six from the mountains, and keep them in readiness for slaughtering the instant that death should take place. When slaughtered, a portion of the meat is sent to their different neighbours, which is considered as equivalent to requiring the attendance of the individual at the interment of the deceased; and after this is accomplished, the whole party return and feast on the remainder until it is either consumed or carried away. The hides are tanned, and sent to Muscat for sale. The whole number at present on the island is about sixteen hundred.

    Vast flocks of sheep and goats are found in every part of the island; the latter are indeed so numerous that the owners keep no account of them. The sheep have not the enormous tail which disfigures those of Arabia and Egypt; they are usually small and lean, with very slender legs, and their flesh is not well tasted. The Bedouins wash them every three months to prevent their getting the rot; their wool is afterwards manufactured into the thick cloaks so well known in Arabia and Persia. The goats are of several varieties, one a milch goat, of which nearly equal care is taken with the sheep; another of a reddish colour, with long shaggy hair, which is permitted to rove unmolested and unattended about the island, and appears to be common property; a third, the wild goat, which is only found in the loneliest glens, near the loftiest mountains - its flesh is much prized by the Bedouins. When the shepherds are desirous of catching them, they seek the track by which they pass up and down the mountains; across this they spread a net; and one of their number then ascends to the summit of the mountain by another route, and makes his appearance before the animal, who no sooner discovers him than he darts down the path, and becomes entangled in the net, when he is quickly secured by those stationed there for that purpose. Amidst the hills over Hadibu, and on the plain contiguous to it, there are a great number of asses which were described to me as differing from the domestic ass; but after repeated opportunities of observing them, I could find no reason for such a distinction. The introduction of camels having superseded the necessity of employing them as beasts of burden, they are permitted by their-masters to stray where they please, and now wander about in troops of 10 or 12, evincing little fear unless approached very near, when they dart away with much rapidity. Though not applied by the natives to any useful purpose, yet they would no doubt be found serviceable, should occasion again require it. The only wild animals known amidst the hills are civet cats. They are very numerous, and were frequently brought to me for sale, but I could not learn that the natives collect the perfume. I kept one for some time; it was a female, and measured 2 feet 9 inches, including the tail, which was 9 ½ inches. Its hair was long and not very fine, its colour dark grey, streaked with vertical bars of black; the head small and handsome, resembling in that as well as in the length of its neck and body the mangousta; it was always fed on rats, and would take five or six of these out of the cage, or trap, in which they were caught and brought to it, and kill them instantly. The fore legs were short and black, with five separate and strong toes on each foot; the hinder legs were much longer and of the same colour. It seized its prey with its mouth, but used its fore paws with much dexterity. While chasing its prey it frequently used its tail in assisting itself to turn or leap on such occasions I have seen it strike the ground with so much force as to cause the tail to bleed at the extremity. Its temper was in general good: but when provoked it exhibited much ferocity. I kept this animal for about three months; he died from the damp weather in the monsoon at Bombay. Hyenas, jackals, monkeys, and other animals, which are common to the shores of either continent, are unknown here; we do not even find the antelope, a circumstance the more singular, as they abound in the islands off the Arabian coast. Dogs are also unknown, and one we had on board was frequently mistaken by the natives for a pig. I saw but one snake during my stay on the island, and the head of that was too much bruised for me to ascertain if it was poisonous, but the natives assured me that it was. From them I also learned that after the rains a great many make their appearance, and some marvellous stories were told me respecting their size and fierceness. On the low land we found an astonishing number of scorpions, centipedes, and a large and venomous description of spider called *nargub* by the Arabs-the bite of which creates alarming inflammation, and even with young children death. In some parts of the island, on the plains, it was a chance, if a stone was turned over, but that one or more of these insects would be found underneath. Locusts have been rarely seen in Socotra. Ants are very numerous, and the bite of one kind is scarcely less painful than the sting of a wasp. Near the pearl millet inclosures field-mice are often observed; and on the hills rats and other vermin are common. The chameleon is a native of the island: the natives frequently brought them to me for sale, and some were larger than I had before seen. The only birds we saw were crows, wild ducks, a species of water fowl with red legs and dark plumage, woodpigeons (numerous), swallows, lap-wings, owls, bats, and four different species of vulture, the last particularly useful in clearing the earth of carcases and filth. There is also a small bird with a red beak and dark purple plumage, called in the Socotran language '*Mahuarad*,' which utters a shrill and loud cry not unlike that which might be produced by an effort of the human voice. Cassawaries are said to have been seen on the island as well as flamingos; I have seen the latter passing over, but never the former.

Government - It has been already noticed that the government of the Island of Socotra was from a very early period dependent on: the kings of the Incense country; and the early Portuguese navigators found them, on their first arrival, still in the undisturbed possession of their ancient patrimony. When Albuquerque conquered the island he vested its government in the hands of some of his officers, who, with a remnant of his troops, were left behind to retain it; but the Portuguese sway was short; they speedily intermarried with the inhabitants, lost their ascendancy, and Socotra again resumed its dependence on its ancient masters. From this period until within the last half century a brother, or some near relation of the sultan of Qishn, on the Arabian coast, resided constantly on the island as its governor; but it is now merely subjected to an annual visit from such a personage. The revenue is then collected, and any complaints which require the interference of the Sultan are brought before him. During our stay at Qishn and on the island we made numerous inquiries to ascertain who at present exercises this power; but it proved no easy matter to discover this. The old Sultan being blind and incapable of managing the affairs of his government, various claimants appeared; but one, Abdullah, being pointed out as the influential individual, we procured from him the letters which specified the nature of our visit, and required the islanders to render us any assistance we might stand in need of. As already seen, however, little attention was paid to these letters, and during our stay another chief, Hamed ben Tary, arrived, and under threat of burning the town, succeeded at Qalansiyah in procuring about thirty dollars worth of ghee. He also sent directions to Hadibu, forbidding our being furnished with camels or guide; and again departing for Qishn, boasted of what he had done; After him no other member of the family was expected on the island; and as the sum collected annually barely exceeds in value 200 dollars, the authority of the Sultan may be considered more nominal than real. Abdullah, in his visits, has been known to inflict chastisement with his own hand on the Bedouins who neglected to bring him the full quantity of ghee to which he considered himself entitled, and even to imprison them for a few days; but I could not learn that he possessed sufficient power to inflict punishment of any kind on the Arabs, the greater number of whom are indeed exempt from contributions. It is from those who collect ghee at Hadibu, Qalansiyah, and Qadub, that he obtains this only article which he now draws from the island.

The attention of Abdullah during his annual visit being now wholly directed towards this collection of revenue, though complaints from former usage are occasionally brought before him, yet the instances are rare, and his decisions are not much attended to. At Hadibu, an old Arab, who was formerly a Sepoy in the service of Bajee Rao, by virtue of his age and long residence in the town possesses some influence. Another at Qalansiyah, named Salem, is also qualified by the townsmen with the title of Sheikh, in order mainly, it would appear, that he may receive presents from vessels visiting the port; but, altogether, nothing is more certain than that they do not possess throughout the island a constituted authority either civil or military, or of any description whatsoever.

Notwithstanding the singular anomaly of so great a number of people residing together without any chiefs or laws, offences against the good order of society appear infinitely less frequent than among more civilized nations. theft, murder, and other heinous crimes, are almost unknown; and no stronger instance can be given of the absence of the former than them fact of my wandering for two months on the island without having during that period missed the most trifling article. Some intelligent natives, also, assured me that the only disturbances known were occasional quarrels among the Bedouins respecting their pasture grounds; which were usually settled either by the individuals fighting the matter out with sticks, or by the interference of their friends.

It is, no doubt, this security of person and property that has brought so many settlers from the continents on either side to the island. Beyond the patriarchal authority hereafter noticed, there does not appear to be any subordinate rank or distinction; and all are respectable in proportion to their wealth in flocks and herds. That the Socotrans possess no maritime enterprise is at once shown by their having no boats; yet they do not appear averse to commercial pursuits; and the voyager who may have to transact business with them will find to his cost, unless he be somewhat wary, that their talents for selling and bartering are not contemptible. The wants of those who reside on the island are, however, so few and so easily satisfied, that they have but little motive to stimulate them to more industrious pursuits; and I question if, under the name and protection of their Arab chiefs (notwithstanding their occasional rapacity), they do not enjoy more liberty and ease in the indulgence of their natural indolence than they would do if placed under more active rulers. The doctrines of the Koran, which are widely and generally disseminated amongst them, are not calculated to remove their apathetic habits.

Population-The inhabitants of the island may be divided into two different classes, those who inhabit the mountains, and the high land near the western extremity of the island, who, there is every reason to believe, are the aborigines - and those who reside in Hadibu, Qalansiyah, Qadub, and the eastern end of the island. The latter are a mongrel race, the descendants of Arabs, African slaves, Portuguese, and several other nations: of the former, or Bedouins, I shall give as full a description as my materials will admit, - premising, however, that although from personal observation I have been enabled to procure every necessary information connected with the present physical habits and domestic manners of this isolated race, yet on some interesting points connected with their former condition, religion, and usages, on which I was anxious to obtain some knowledge, I found this impossible from the jealous and suspicious character of those with whom I was obliged to converse. They either declined answering my questions altogether, or made replies calculated to mislead.

The Arabs who visit Socotra, in consequence of the pastoral habits of this class, and their wandering mode of life, bestow on them the appellation of Bedouins: to which race, though they differ widely from them in some points, they have yet in others a striking resemblance. The principles of their political constitution are exceedingly simple; all are divided into families or tribes, each occupying a determined domain on the island, and each having a representative or head who formerly exercised what might be termed a patriarchal authority over them. In general, the office is hereditary, though it is sometimes filled by persons who have been selected for the superiority of their abilities.

It was to this individual that the Sultan formerly, when he resided on the island, looked for the collection of his tribute; and to the Sultan he was also in some measure answerable for the good conduct of his tribe; but at present his authority appears to be merely that of an influential individual, before whom complaints are taken for arbitration, but who possesses no power to punish a delinquent. An individual may also carry his complaint before the Sultan or his deputy, or he may, which is the usual practice, retaliate on the injurer or any member of his family; but these affairs are not carried to the sanguinary length they are in Arabia, where the murder of an individual is revenged on the persons of his assassins or their relatives. I made numerous inquiries, but could not ascertain that their quarrels ever terminated in death to either party; which may, in some measure, be owing to their having neither fire-arms nor weapons of any other description excepting sticks and stones. But, at the same time, their peaceable habits are forcibly illustrated by the fact of so many tribes occupying territories intermingled with each other, where the valuable nature of pasturage, and the scarcity of water, compel them from different quarters to meet at the same spot without reference to the actual owners; and that yet skirmishing amongst them is of rarest occurrence.

Physical appearance of the Mountaineers-The men are usually tall, with strong, muscular, and remarkably well-formed limbs, a facial angle as open as that of Europeans, the nose slightly aquiline, the eyes lively and expressive, the teeth good, and the mouth well formed. Their hair is worn long, and curls naturally; but, unlike that of the inhabitants of Madagascar and several of the Asiatic islands, without approach to a woolly or crisp texture. They also generally wear a beard and whiskers, but never moustaches. They have no characteristics in common with the Arabs or Somaulees; and some points about them are even essentially different. Their complexion varies a good deal, some being as fair as the inhabitants of Surat, while others are as dark as the Hindoos on the banks of the Ganges. They walk with an erect gait over the worst ground, and bound over the hills like antelopes. From constantly climbing the rocks and mountains, they have contracted a habit of turning in their toes, which gives them when on the plains a slight degree of awkwardness in their walk; yet, notwithstanding this slight defect, the regularity of their features, the fairness of their complexions, (for those which are dark are but a small portion of their number,) and the models of symmetry which they occasionally present to the eye, render them a remarkably good-looking people, distinct and removed from any of the varieties of the human race seen on the shores of the continent on either side. Their dress consists of a piece of cloth wrapped round their waist, with the end thrown over the shoulders, but without ornaments; in their girdle is placed a knife; and, as they have no weapons, they carry in their hands a large stick. In their various modes of dressing the hair they display a little foppery-some having it frizzled like that of the Bisharee Arabs on the coast of Egypt, others allowing it to curl naturally, while the greater part permit it to grow to a considerable length, and plait it into tresses confined to the head' by a braided cord made from their own hair. Their skins are clear, shining, and remarkably free from eruption or cutaneous disorders. Many are, however, scarred from the application of hot irons for the removal of local complaints, a mode of cure they are as fond of practising as their neighbours the Arabs of the continent.

The same remarks may be applied with little alteration to the persons and features of the females. We find in them the same symmetry of form, the same regularity of feature, and the same liveliness of expression; but their complexion does not vary in an equal degree, few being darker than the fairest of the men, and some, especially when young, being remarkably pretty. The legs of some of those advanced in age are of an astonishing thickness; but this defect is chiefly observable among those who reside in the low lands, and seldom occurs among the highland females. Their dress consists of a cloak, (*camaline*) [4] bound round their waist by a leathern girdle, and a kind of wrapper of Dungaree cloth which is thrown over their shoulders. Round their necks they wear necklaces made of red coral, coloured glass, amber, with sometimes a string of dollars to each ear; they wear also three, and sometimes four, ear-rings made of silver, and about three inches diameter; two are worn on the upper, and one on the lower part of the ear. They go unveiled, and whenever we approached their houses conversed freely with us.

Habitations. - In a moist climate like Socotra, it would be impossible for several months to live in tents; and as the variation of the seasons compels the Bedouins to shift with their flocks in search of pasturage, it may be considered a bountiful provision of nature that they are, in the numerous natural excavations with which the limestone hills abound, provided with habitations ready fashioned to their hands. A Bedouin merely selects such one of these as from its size and situation seems best calculated for his purpose, then by means of loose stones portions off different apartments for himself and family within it, and the remainder is left to afford shelter for his flocks. Singular spots are thus occasionally chosen for these places of abode. I have seen them in the face of a nearly vertical hill, at a height of 800 feet from the plain; but in the valleys they have another description of dwelling-place. The rocks here, wherever limestone occurs, are equally cavernous with the hills. A cave is accordingly selected, of which they widen, if necessary, the entrance so as to allow it to open into an inclosure; the upper part is then covered over with rafters, on which turf and some earth is placed, so that it becomes difficult at a short distance to distinguish it from the surrounding country; and a wall of loose stones incloses a circular space about thirty yards in diameter in the immediate vicinity, which serves at night as a fold for their sheep and goats. I visited the interior of several of these. The only furniture they contained was a stone for grinding corn, some skins on which to sleep, other skins for holding water and milk, some earthen cooking pots, and a few cloaks [5] hanging on lines tied across the roof. In one of these, tied by the four corners, and suspended from a peg by a string, will frequently be seen a child sleeping; and this contrivance serves also as a cradle, being swung to and fro when they wish to compose its tenant to sleep. In hot weather, when the ground is parched with heat, these caves are of a clammy coldness. The Bedouins are by no means particular in keeping them clean; and they usually swarm with fleas and other vermin. The mildness of the climate renders a fireplace unnecessary, and that which is required for culinary purposes is lighted outside. The closeness of the interior, as they have no other opening than the door, would otherwise I believe be intolerable.

The men pass their time in tending their flocks, in collecting Dragon's Blood and aloes, and in occasional visits to the towns, where the two latter, with their ghee, are exchanged for dates, *pearl millet [6]* (the *sorgo* of Egypt, *jowaree* of India), and clothes. Accustomed to traverse their mountains from childhood, they perform on these occasions journeys of thirty or forty miles, climbing almost perpendicular precipices, and crossing deep ravines without apparently experiencing any fatigue or inconvenience. The principal employment of the females abroad is also looking after the flocks; at home they make ghee, card and spin wool, which they afterwards weave into cloaks, and attend to their domestic duties: in addition to which, the other toils consequent on their pastoral mode of life, as with most barbarous nations, fall principally on them; and I have frequently seen them at the close of the day, after securing their flocks, proceed, with their children on their backs, a distance of several miles, to fill and bring home skins of water, while their husbands have remained with no other occupation than smoking or sleeping. They have a curious method of cleaning their wool. They place it in a heap on the floor; and hold a bow over it, the string of which they snap against it till all the dust has flown off. Their method of weaving is also very simple, but a description of it without a figure would be unintelligible. As it is difficult for them to procure steel, they have recourse to a method of obtaining combustion practised by several savage nations. They procure two pieces of wood, the one hard (*Ziziphus spina-christi* if procurable), the other a short flat lath from a date branch. The former is twelve inches long, and is inserted in a hollow formed for the purpose in the latter. The stick is then twirled briskly between the two palms, pressing it at the same time with some force, until the dust ground out by the attrition (and which escapes down the side by a small groove) ignites; it is then placed on a palm branch, and flame is produced. They have a method of obtaining a whiff of tobacco equally simple. They slip off a branch of the *Hildebrandt's boxwood* -tree of the required length and thickness for the tube, and cut the extremity of this as we do a quill before splitting it; this part then serves as a bowl in which the tobacco is placed, while a small wooden plug, having a hole in its centre, at once prevents it from ascending the tube, and at the same time permits the smoke to be inhaled.

The Bedouins subsist chiefly on milk, and on the grain and dates which they receive in exchange for their ghee; when occasion calls for a feast, or a visitor arrives, a goat or sheep is killed. Their mode of cooking is very simple. They separate the meat from the bones, cut it into small pieces, and boil the whole in an earthen pot. They use no dishes, and the meat is placed on a small mat, round which they sit. In eating, contrary to the usual *Muslim* custom, they cut their meat with knives, which are procured from Whalers and other vessels that touch at the island.

Character and Manners - The moral character of the Bedouins stands high; and the rare occurrence of heinous crimes among them has been already noticed. In general, they may be considered as a lively, generous race; but the most distinguishing trait of their character is their hospitality, which is practised alike by all, and is only limited by the means of the individual called on to exercise it. Nor is this, as with the Socotran Arabs, confined to those of their own faith; and while with the latter we were unceasingly tired by silly questions relating either to our religion or our views on the island, the Bedouins gave themselves no concern either about the one or the other. Ever cheerful they were always ready to enter into conversation, or to be pleased with what was shown them. I saw no instrument of music during our stay on the island, but they appear passionately fond of song; and on one occasion, at a wedding, I saw them, as has been noticed in the narrative, engaged in dancing. The Bedouins have a great variety of modes of salutation. Two friends meeting will kiss each other on the cheek or shoulder, six or eight times, then shake hands, kiss them, and afterwards interchange a dozen sentences of compliment. They have also the same singular and indelicate mode of salutation which is practised at Qishn, where they place their noses together, and accompany the action by drawing up their breath audibly through the nostrils at the same time. Male and female relations salute each other in public, in this manner; those of different sexes, who are merely known to each other, kiss each the other's shoulder, except in the case of the principal individual of the tribe, whose knees the females salute, while he returns the compliment on their forehead. The old men salute children in the same manner.

Language, &c. - I am not sufficiently versed in oriental literature, to ascertain what affinity the Socotran language may bear to the Arabic or any other language; I have therefore subjoined a vocabulary of words in most general use among the Bedouins, by which I trust the scholar may be able to proceed in an inquiry that can scarcely fail to lead to interesting results. I may notice in passing that the mountaineers from the Arabian coast are sometimes able to make themselves well understood by the Bedouins of Socotra; but the Arabs from Muscat, or from any of the neighbouring towns, are quite unable to do so.

The Socotran language is in general use even by those who have permanently settled on the island; and Arabic is only spoken by the merchants when transacting business with the traders who arrive in their *Baghlas*.

At as late a period as when the Portuguese visited Socotra they found on it books, written in the Chaldean character [7]. I hoped consequently to be able to procure some manuscripts or books which might serve to throw light on the history of the island; but in answer to repeated inquiries regarding such, I was always assured that some, which they acknowledged to have possessed, they left in their houses when they fled to the hills, and that the Wahhabis, during their visit, destroyed or carried them off. The former is the most probable, as these sectaries, in the genuine spirit of Omar's precept, value only one book.

With the use of the compass the Bedouins are totally unacquainted; and they have no terms in their language by which to express the cardinal points. The superiority of the Arabic numerals over their own has induced them entirely to discontinue the use of the latter; and in all transactions among themselves, as well as with the Arabs, the former are now used. It was thus not without some difficulty that I was able to collect the Socotra numerals. They are as follows: 1, *kaud*: 2, *tereau*: 3, *thadder*: 4, *erubah*: 5, *hamish*: 6, *ieitah*: 7, *heybah*: 8, *tomany*: 9, *seah*: 10, *usharee*: 11, *nsharee kaud*, that is 10 and 1: 12, *nsharee tereau*, that is 10 and 2: and so on to 20, which is *usharoo*: and 21, which is *usharoo kaud*: 30, which is *thadder ushar*, or three tens: 40, *erubah usharee* or four tens, to a hundred, which is *mieh*. But by this decimal mode of calculation they could advance no farther than ten hundred; and I have frequently inquired, without success, for some term to express a thousand. This gives no very high opinion of their mental capacity, and it furnishes, unless they have sadly retrograded, a strong proof also of their never having made any considerable progress in civilization [8].

Diseases-During my stay in Socotra I saw but few cases of illness. Four of cancer, and as many of elephantiasis, were brought to me for medical assistance. A hard and painful swelling of the abdomen, brought on by irregularity in diet, was frequent; but this was not surprising, as a Bedouin will live for several days on milk and a little pearl millet [9]- and then feast to excess on a sheep, the flesh of which is but half boiled. Some bad sores were shown me, occasioned by punctures from the thorns of the *Ziziphus spina-christi*; [10] but in general diseases are of very rare occurrence, and the Bedouins may be considered a hardy and healthy race. In the most solitary and lonely ravines and valleys, I occasionally met with idiots who were permitted to stray about by themselves. Food is given them when they approach any habitation;

but they usually subsist either on the wild herbs, which they gather on the mountains, or on the wild goats, which they knock on the head with stones. Near Ras Moree I saw one of these men going about perfectly naked; I came on him unexpectedly, but he fled with much celerity, the instant he saw me.

Customs. - Of the many peculiar customs which existed before the introduction of Islam (Mahomedanism), a few only are now retained, of which the most singular is, that they do not circumcise their children until they are past the age of puberty, while, with other Muslims this is performed at a very early age. On the eastern part of the island, amidst the mountains, I was shown a rude stone-chair, in which it is customary for the Bedouins to seat their youths (who are sometimes brought from a long distance) while the operation is performed.

They have preserved the remembrance of a singular trial by ordeal formerly practised. An individual supposed to have been guilty of any heinous crime was placed, bound hand and foot, on the summit of some eminence, and there compelled to remain three days. If rain fell during that period on or near him, he was considered guilty, and punished by being stoned to death; but if the weather, on the contrary, continued fair, he was acquitted.

Some popular traditions were related to me, but they appeared so little peculiar or characteristic as scarcely to be worth transcription. They have a story that there is a class of women who, like the Gouls of Arabia, lie in ambush in lone and secret places to catch and devour the weary traveller; and so prevalent is this belief that I have heard both Arabs and Bedouins maintain that a greater number of deaths occurred in this way than in any other. The gravity indeed with which this opinion was maintained, even by the more enlightened of the natives, surprised me a good deal; neither ridicule nor argument had any effect in shaking their faith in it. The only probable origin I could assign to a tale so absurd, was that the bodies of the mountaineers, who fall occasionally from the rock, are sometimes found to be partly devoured by vultures and other birds of prey; and the love of the horrible and marvellous may induce them to ascribe this to the agency of evil spirits.

At first sight it may appear singular that while, as will be shown in the subsequent section, the population of the eastern coast of the Island is mixed and varied, that of the western still continues pure, and presents the same characteristics. But the causes. on examination, are obvious. The Bedouins make no scruple to give their daughters to the native Arabs, and even to visitors who may pass but a short time on the island; and these departing with their husbands, their sons naturally follow the avocation of their fathers, and rarely, if ever, return to the pastoral pursuits of their maternal progenitors; while the females again are not married to Bedouins, for the Arabs, though they have no objection to take a Bedouin wife, would hold themselves disgraced were they to marry their daughters to any but those of their own class. This, then, in some degree, accounts for the circumstance in question; but independently of this as one cause, the want of water, felt during the greater part of the year, on the western part of the island and its general sterility, offer so little inducement to the native Arabs to reside there, that with the exception of some huts on the sea-coast, in which they take up their quarters for the purpose of fishing, i did not, in my journeying in that part, meet half-a-dozen families. And there is thus no intermixture because there is no immigration.

But of those who are comprehended under the name of Bedouins there are a few distinct tribes, of which it is necessary that separate mention should be made. Those most worthy of attention are a small tribe of about 150 men, called Bahee Rahow, in the vicinity of Ras Moree. Their forefathers are said to have been Jews, and the features of the tribe still retain a strong resemblance to those of that race. The Saymee, the Sayfee, the Dirmee, and the Zirzhee, are, in like manner, said to be descended from the Portuguese, and are known under the general appellation of Camhane or Camhan. They occupy the granite mountains, are rich in flocks of sheep and cows, and though the resemblance to the European cast of countenance may still be traced, and in some cases they have even preserved their original name, yet they exhibit none of those symptoms of physical degradation which are observable in the race of Portuguese in India, on the contrary, some of the finest figures and most intelligent people I saw on the island were of this class. Though readily recognised by the other tribes, their descent appears in no way to be considered as a reproach to them. It ' was said that a few families in the mountains continued to speak even their original language, but I never fell in with any such. Some of the hills on the east and north side of the island still, however, retain the appellations bestowed upon them by Portuguese.

Island Arabs-As I have preserved the name of Bedouin bestowed on the mountain-tribes, without regard to the general signification of the term, I shall also retain the name of Arabs, with which the remainder, with no higher claim, have invested themselves. Under this designation, are included those who occupy Hadibu, the villages of Qadub and Qalansiyah, and the greater part of the eastern portion of the island. They may all be classed as foreigners, or the descendants of foreigners, who have settled there. The principal part are Arabs, left by boats passing between Zanzibar and the Arabian coast to dispose of cargoes, and who marry and remain permanently; the others are Indians, Somalis (Somaulees), Arabian slaves, &c., who are attracted hither by various motives. preserve the recollection of their original country, and for this purpose, subjoin its name to their own. Thus our guide was called Suleiman Muscaty, or Suleiman from Muscat. Though so mixed a class, the Socotran Arabs all wear the same dress, and have adopted the same language and customs. Their colour, features, and figure, as may be expected from their various descents, are so varied that it is impossible to speak of them in any general terms, they have, in fact, every grade, from the flattened nose, thick lip, and woolly head of the negro, to the equally well-known characteristics of the Arabs. Their dress consists of a loose single shirt descending below the knees, which is confined to the waist by a leathern girdle, to which are suspended all the arms they can muster. The lower classes wear nothing but a piece of striped linen, with another thrown over their shoulders when they are exposed to the sun. In rainy or cold weather they all wear a thick woollen coat sufficiently large completely to envelope them. The female dress consists of a long chemise of Indian cloth, with a loose wrapper over it; the ends of which, being drawn round their person, are brought up to the neck in order to serve as a veil when they desire to conceal their face.

The employments of the Socotran Arabs are either tending their date-groves and flocks, making ghee, or trading between Muscat and Zanzibar. Their date-groves give them but little trouble, for as soon as the owner can scrape together enough money he buys a slave to attend upon them; and if his wealth increases, he adds to the number both of slaves and trees. Traders proceed among the mountains on camels, taking with them various articles which they exchange for ghee; the quantity collected is very great; I was assured that in some seasons it amounts to 2500 measures. The Arabs who engage in the trade to Zanzibar with this article receive in exchange for it grain and slaves; and, contrary to the custom of the east, the Socotran Arabs treat their slaves with great harshness; they work them hard, and feed and clothe them but indifferently. As their pursuits can only be engaged in during the fair or N.E. monsoon, it follows that a considerable portion of their time is passed without employment of any kind; to obviate the tedium of which period, I did not observe that they have recourse to games of chance or amusement of any description. Their time appears spent in visiting each other, drinking coffee, smoking and sleeping. In place of taking up their abodes in caves, as the Bedouins do, the Arabs, who reside outside the towns, live in huts which are mostly of a circular form, the walls being constructed of loose stones and cemented with mortar, of which mud is the principal ingredient. They are rarely more than four feet in height, inclosing a space of from twelve to fourteen feet diameter; and are sometimes surmounted by a conical roof projecting nearly a foot over the sides, constructed of the branches of date-trees, and plastered at the apex in order to prevent the rain getting through. In other cases, the walls are built of the same height, and rafters are laid across them in a horizontal direction, covered with date-branches, and cemented over with lime and sometimes turf. The goats may then frequently be observed grazing on the vegetation growing out of the latter. In several of those which I visited, in which It was impossible to stand upright, which were swarming with fleas, and which in size, it will be remembered, are scarcely larger than an English pigstye, two or three families, each consisting of four or five individuals, resided together. It is not therefore a matter of surprise that fever sometimes sweeps off a whole hamlet. Were the materials, of which these wretched and unseemly buildings are constructed, scarce, and only to be procured with difficulty, we might pardon the little attention to comfort, accommodation, or health, which their construction exhibits; but when these are abundant, and there are better models in the town before them, it furnishes a strong proof of their sloth and indolence, that they are thus indifferently lodged; and with many other circumstances, this may be considered as showing that they have little capacity or inclination for improvement.

Though the Bedouins are healthy, the Arabs seem a weak and sickly race. Dangerous fevers are said to prevail among them after the rains; and the graves in the vicinity of Hadibu are frightfully numerous: so that it may be truly said of that town, that it contains treble the number of houses that it does of inhabitants; and ten times the number of tombs that it does of both. On other parts of the island, wherever vestiges of former habitations could be traced, there might also be seen the same proportion of graves. The Arabs formerly paid great attention to their tombs. Of the tombstones, one was placed at the head, another at the feet, and a third in the centre; and on the first were inscribed the name, age, &c. of the deceased. But the Wahhabi, from their aversion to any kind of decoration over the remains of the dead, broke and destroyed the whole of these which came under their notice during their stay.

Religion.-My attention was particularly directed towards obtaining information respecting their forms of religion. At present, every individual on the island is, or professes himself to be, a *Muslim*; but the Bedouins, as in Arabia, hold their tenets but loosely. Many neglect the fast of the Ramadan; and few are acquainted with the morning and evening prayers-those few rarely troubling themselves with repeating them. Circumcision, as already noticed, is not practised until a late period; and, in some families, I have reason to believe it is omitted altogether. The Socotran Arabs, on the contrary, are zealous professors of the *Muslim* faith, though at the same time utterly ignorant of its most essential doctrines; and, like all those nations who possess but a slight knowledge of their tenets, they are bigoted and intolerant to an insufferable degree. During my stay in Socotra some individuals of the survey occasionally fell sick, and the horror they expressed on these occasions at the idea of its becoming necessary to bury a Christian on the island, convinced me, that if it was ever done, they would perform their threat of disinterring the corpse with every indignity, and throwing it into the sea.

The Mahrah Arabs, from the coast of Arabia, a noble race, who occasionally reside for a few months on the island, ridicule them for this spirit of intolerance, and assured us, even in the presence of the zealots, that the Socotrans were poor wretches, who had nothing to plead in defence of it, save the lowest state of Ignorance and their mongrel descent. After the receipt of Ahmed ben-Tary's letter, prohibiting our further progress through the interim of the island, and when I was confined by the Socotran Arabs for several days in the town, it was principally through the influence of the Mahrah Arabs, exercised on that occasion, that I was again enabled to set forward on my journey. The behaviour of then former on all similar occasions exhibited a mixture of irresolution, timidity, and avarice, which I have never seen equalled. They wavered between dread of the Sheikh, if they permitted us to go, and fear of missing what they might gain by hiring out their camels, if they prevented us. Exorbitant demands were thus made; and when they found I would not listen to these, they continued to hold councils for three days, during which I had all packed up in readiness for starting. Permission was given and refused more than half a dozen times.

It is observed by Malte Brun, in his 'Universal Geography,' that the population of this island might form a subject of lengthened discussion. He notices, on the authority of Philostorgius, Edrisi, and Hamdoullah, that a colony, sent by Alexander the Great, remained here for a long period; that during the time of Philostorgins (an ecclesiastical historian, who wrote a history of the Church, on Arian principles, at the conclusion of the fourth century), they spoke the Syriac language: and he cites various other authorities to prove the existence of a race of Christians by whom the island was peopled until as late a period as 1593, when the Nestorians and Jacobites had each a bishop residing on it. Even when Sir Thomas Roe visited it in 1612, he observes, "that the Bediognes," as he styles them, "were of the Nestorian persuasion." In the absence of books or manuscripts of any description (for I believe no notices connected with the habits, religion, or character of these islanders have been handed down since this period to Europeans), it might prove a hazardous task to venture to state, on the faith of their own traditions only, any of the causes or events which have led to the now total abolition of the Christian, and establishment of the Mahomedan faith: information on these points may probably be gained from authors to which I have not at present any means of gaining access. But I cannot altogether dismiss the subject without observing, that as the channel of the Indian trade, at the early period to which the above-mentioned author refers, was by way of Socotra and the ports in the Red Sea, it is not so extraordinary, in fact, as it may at first sight appear, that Christianity should have been thus early established here.

Sale observes, in his 'Preliminary Discourse,' "that the persecutions and disorders which happened in the Eastern Church soon after the beginning of the third century, obliged great numbers of Christians to seek shelter in the country of liberty (Arabia); who being for the most part of the Jacobite community, that sect generally prevailed among the Arabs." And although it does not appear that the southern parts of the Peninsula were subjected to the ecclesiastical rule of either the Nestorian or Jacobite bishops, yet, from the circumstances above adverted to, it is not probable that they would have overlooked a spot like Socotra, where there is every reason to believe they could indulge unmolested in the open profession of their faith. With respect to the disappearance of these primitive Christians, as well as those which were left on the island by the Portuguese, it may be observed too, that it would be an anomaly in human nature, almost as striking as that afforded by the history of the Jews, if, surrounded as they were by natives universally professing the *Muslim* religion, receiving no fresh influx from those of their own persuasion, and left as an isolated and neglected race, they had refrained from embracing the new doctrines. That this was accomplished by a silent and gradual change, and not by any violent or exterminating measures, appears evident by the simple fact of their descendants existing as a distinct race to the present day; and evidence as to the fact of numerous colonies, of different nations or persuasions, having formerly existed on the island, may be found in the present arrangement and distribution of its families into tribes, many of which are still recognized as of foreign origin.

TIME HAS NOT PRODUCED A GREATER CHANGE IN THE GOVERNMENT OR constitution of this island than it has in its ecclesiastical arrangement. In place of one archbishop and two bishops, there is now but a single priest, who combines in his own person the various offices of *moollah* [religious leader], *muezzin* [prayer caller], and schoolmaster. A single *qadi* solemnizes the whole of the marriages which take place throughout the island, and I have, on more than one occasion, met Bedouins seeking him for a certificate when he has been about on the hills cultivating his date-groves. Two small and insignificant mosques at Hadibu, and one yet smaller at Qalansiyah, are now the only places of worship for the reception of the faithful. It would form a curious subject of inquiry what form of religion the establishment of the Christian faith displaced. A ruinous building was shown me which was said to have been an ancient place of worship; but it was in too dilapidated a state to enable me to ascertain the truth of the tradition; nor did I discover others that threw any light on the subject.

The population of the island, as stated by some travellers at one thousand souls, is evidently much under-rated. From their wandering mode of life and other causes it was difficult, from any inspection of the island, to form a correct inference of the population of the whole; but the method I adopted was, at the conclusion of each day, to note the number of individuals I had seen, and these amounted in all to above two thousand. I am confident, however, that this does not comprehend half their number, for in several places they concealed themselves whenever we approached; and though my ramble led me to many parts of the island, yet there were necessarily many hills and remote valleys which I could not inspect. I am further strengthened in this belief by summing up the number of the tribes; and, on the whole, I fix the amount of the population at four thousand. Two intelligent Arabs, who have resided on the island upwards of ten years, and have journeyed to many parts of it, tell me they consider even this below the actual number; but with Arabs an allowance should always be made for numerical exaggerations. Comparing this calculation with the surface of the island, which amounts to about one thousand square miles, it gives four individuals to each square mile; which, when we reflect on the great proportion of bare rock which it exhibits, appears very considerable.

Although I made diligent search and constant inquiries, I was unable (with the exception of those which mark the stay of the Portuguese) to discover any ancient vestiges or monuments that would prove the island to have been peopled by a race further advanced than the present. I think, however, that there is reason to believe the population must have been at one time more numerous; and that the island was consequently better cultivated. It is impossible to ascertain at what period the number was reduced; but that they have not been exempt from contagion, or some other occasional scourge, appears evident from the existence of such a multitude of graves on every part of the island, many of which appear to have been constructed at the same time. On the other hand, that this period is somewhat remote, is equally evident, not only by the total disappearance of all such traces of improvement on the face of the country, but by the present condition of the inhabitants. It must not be referred to the period immediately preceding the visit of the Wahhabis (as has been suggested in some discussions relating to the island), for those fierce sectaries confined their outrages, and the extent of their devastation, to Hadibu and its vicinity; and they did not attempt to pursue the inhabitants who fled to the mountains on the first intimation of their approach.

CHAPTER 9
LANGUAGE

LANGUAGE 97

The following Words and Phrases in the *Socotran* and *Arabic* are given as a Specimen of the Language of that Island*.

كلام انعرب   كلام اهل جزيره سقطري

ARABIC.		SOCOTRAN.	
طويل	ríyau	ريڍُو	Tall. Long.
قصير	karhaï	كرهِي	Short.
ماي بحر	Riyoh réh'n	ريه رنهن	Salt Water.
ماي حلو	Riyoh ḥáli	ريه حالي	Sweet or Fresh Water
ماي اشرب	Riyoh larí	ريه لري	Water to drink.
اكل	aṣtah	استه	To eat.
بيت	kár	قار	A House.
بلاد	chírhaï	چيرهِي	Town.
سيف	eshukkó	اشكو	Sword.
تفق	bandúk (Ar.)	بندوق	A Musket.
رصاص	Raṣáṣ (Ar.)	رصاص	Musket-ball (lead.)
حديد	haṣ-hen	حصهن	Iron.
صفر	ṣafar (Ar.)	صفر	Copper.
حطب	ṭerab	طيرب	Wood.
نهار	maṣh-hem	مشهم	Day-time.
ليل	aḥteh	احته	Night-time.
قمر	írah	ايره	The Moon.
نجوم	kókeb (Ar.)	كوكب	The Stars.
شمس	shíhen	شيهن	The Sun.

---

* The Vowels are to be sounded as in *path, there, ravine, whole* and *fuil*: the Consonants as in English, *o* as *u* in *cut, hut*, &c.; *aï* as *i* in *mine*; *au* as *ou* in *thou*; and the dotted letters somewhat more strongly than usual. Each letter has invariably the same sound; and the accents mark the long emphatic syllables. The original was carelessly and inaccurately transcribed: some faults of spelling have been corrected.—S.

ARABIC.		SOCOTRAN.	
تعال	Ta'debah	تعدبه	Come here.
روح	Tetóhar	تنطوهر	Go away.
اجلس	Istaháú (stuhúá?)	استحاو	Sit down.
امشي	ta'add	تعد	Make haste.
ارقد	eïdem	ايدم	To sleep.
اوقف	kassah	قصه	Scarce.
اليوم	har	حر	To-day.
باكر	kérirí	قيريري	To-morrow.
رجال	eïj	عيج	Male.
حرمة	eïchah	عيچه	Female.
ولد	mobyákí	مبياكي	Boy, or Male Infant.
متين	'anąb	عنب	Large Timber.
وصيم	kat'hen	قطهن	Small Timber.
شهر	shahr (Ar.)	شهر	A Month.
شهرين	terá b-shehreïn	ترابشهرين	Two Months.
ثلاثة اشهر	tata'ah shehr	طةعة شهر	Three Months.
اربعة اشهر	arb'ah shehr	اربعه شهر	Four Months.
خمسة اشهر	khúmis shehr	خومس شهر	Five Months.
ستة اشهر	yítah	يية شهر	Six Months.
سبعة اشهر	yibí'ah shehr	يبيعه شهر	Seven Months.
ثمانية اشهر	tamání shehr	تماني اشهر	Eight Months.
تسعة اشهر	sa'ah shehr	سعه شهر	Nine Months.
عشرة اشهر	'ashérah shehr	عشيرة شهر	Ten Months.
حد عشر اشهر	'atíré wotát	عطيري وطات	Eleven Months.
سنه	aïnah	اينه	A Year.
سنتين	terí	تري اينه	Two Years.

LANGUAGE

ARABIC.		SOCOTRAN.	
ثلاثة سنين	ṭaṭa' aïhen	ثلاثة ايهن	Three Years.
اربعه سنين	arba' —	اربع ايهن	Four Years.
خمسه سنين	khémah —	حيمه ايهن	Five Years.
سته سنين	settah —	سته ايهن	Six Years.
سبعه سنين	yibí'ah —	يبيعه ايهن	Seven Years.
ثمان سنين	tamání —	تماني ايهن	Eight Years.
تسعه سنين	sa'ah —	تسعه ايهن	Nine Years.
عشرة سنين	'asherah —	عشرة ايهن	Ten Years
حد عشر سنه	had-'asher —	حد عشر ايهن	Eleven Years.
اثنه عشر سنه	ethná'asher —	اثنه عشر ايهن	Twelve Years.
ثلاثه عشر سنه	telát'asher —	ثلثعشر ايهن	Thirteen Years.
اربعة عشر سنه	arba't'asher —	اربعتعشر ايهن	Fourteen Years.
خمسته عشر سنه	khamsat'asher —	خمسة عشر ايهن	Fifteen Years.
ستعشر سنه	sitt'asher —	ستعشر ايهن	Sixteen Years.
سباتعشر سنه	seb'at'asher —	سبعتعشر ايهن	Seventeen Years.
تمانتعشر سنه	tmanet'asher —	ثمانتعشر ايهن	Eighteen Years.
تستعشر سنه	tis'at'asher —	تسعتعشر ايهن	Nineteen Years.
عشرين سنه	'ashrín —	عشرين ايهن	Twenty Years.
ميه سنه	miyah —	ميه ايهن	One Hundred Years.
الف سنه	alf —	الف ايهن	One Thousand Years.
خيط	shúhaṭ	شوهط	A Fishing-line.
مجدآر	aklahah	اقلهه	A Hook.
بلد	bild	بلد	Sounding-lead.
انجر	barúṣi	بروصي	Anchor.
سلسله	sinsilah (Ar.)	سلسله	A Chain for an anchor.
دقل	dak'har	دقحر	A Mast.

SOCOTRAN.		ARABIC.	
ترمل A Yard.	tarmál	فرمن	
شيرع A Sail.	shíra' (Ar.)	شراع	
ديرة A Compass.	dírah	ديرة	
فانوس A Lantern.	fánús (Ar.)	فانوص	
نبديرة A Flag.	Bindírah (Bandeira. Port.)	بنديرة	
فدهن A Hill, or Mountain.	Fed'han	جبل	
اوبهم A Stone.	Úbehem	حجار	
شرهق At a great distance.	sherhok	بعيد	
شيلي At hand. Close.	shéli	قريت	
شرمهم A Tree, Forest, &c.	Shermuhem	اشجار	
مقديرة Juwárí (Holcus Sorghum.)	Makedírah	الذرة	
بر Corn, or Wheat.	Barr	بر	
دقيق Flour.	dakík (Ar.)	طحين	
ازهر Bread, or Cakes.	ezh-har	خبز	
توترديe Come here!	túterdí	تعال قريب	
توعد شرهف Go away!	tú'ad sherhok	روح بعيد	
تعد سوق Go to Market or Bazaar.	ta'ad sók	روح سوق	
حيرة طهر Go to-day.	heïrah tahr	روح اليوم	
قريرة تحدهن Come to-morrow.	karírah tihdehn	تعال باكر	
ديية Good.	díyah	زين	
ديا Bad.	diyá	شين	
قاط * One.	kát	واحد	
تروة Two.	tarawah	اثنين	

---

* *tát* تاط (v. p. 211.) or *hát* حاط, as in the Ethiopic dialects.—S.

LANGUAGE

ARABIC.		SOCOTRAN.	
ثلاثة	ṭaṭa'ah	ططعة	Three.
اربعة	'arba'ah	اربعه	Four.
خمسة	heïmish	حيمش	Five.
ستة	yítah	ايته	Six.
سبع	yibí'ah	يبيعه	Seven.
ثمان	tamáni	ثماني	Eight.
تسع	sa'ah	سعه	Nine.
عشر	'ashrí	عشري	Ten.
تكلم	ta'ashrí	تعشري	Well-dressed.
عدل	sawù (Ar.)	سوا	Correct, proper, straight.
عوج	kagh'hen	قغهن	Crooked.
كثير	Gaï	كي	Plenty, numerous.
قليل	Ḥarar'hen	حررهن	Few, scarce.
يابس	Táshah	تاشه	Dry.
بنت	Ferhen	فرهن	Daughter, or Female Child.
عجوز	'ajúz (Ar.)	عجوز	Old Woman.
شايب	sheïb	شيب	Old Man.
راس	rí	دي	The Head.
شعر	shiff	شف	The Hair.
جنون	Teri'aïn tefrúz	تري عين تفروز	The Eyebrows.
عين	teï'an	طيعن	The Eyes.
حواجيب	ḥaj-ḥar	حجهر	The Forehead.
اذان	edahn (Ar.)	ادهن	The Ears.
خشم	naḥír	نحير	Nose.
براطم	shíbah	شيبه	The Lips.

101

ARABIC.		SOCOTRAN.	
ضروس	metírmish	مطيرمش	The Teeth.
لسان	lishen	لشن	Tongue.
رقبه	naháshah	نحاشه	The Throat.
كتف	kaurí	كوري	The Shoulders.
ضهر	tádah	طاده	The Back.
بطن	mír	مير	The Stomach.
يد	éyat	ايط	The Arm.
اصابيع	'asábi' (Ar.)	اصابع	The Fingers.
ظفور	Dhafar	ظفر	The Nails.
رجول [ارجل]	s´b	صوب	The Feet.
رز	arhaz	ارهز	Rice.
سمن	Hamí	حمي	Ghí (clarified butter)
زبد	katmír	تطمير	Butter.
حل	salét	صليط	Oil.
حليب	húf	حوف	New Milk.
دجاج	dedáj (Ar.)	دجاج	Fowls.
بيض	beüdh (Ar.)	بيض	Eggs.
غنم	arhen	ارهن	Goats or Sheep.
بقر	elheütein	الهيتين	Cows or Bullocks.
كلب	kelb (Ar.)	كلب	A Dog.
سنور	yirbík	يربوك	The Civet Cat.
بوش	Jemíher	جمي هر	Camels.
غزال	tahrír	طهرير	Antelopes.
لحم	teh	ته	Meat.
سمك	sódah	سوده	Fish.
بصل	Bass'hel (Ar.)	بصهل	Onions.

ARABIC.		SOCOTRAN.	
صراج	Siráj (Ar.)	صراج	A Light, of a candle, lamp, &c.
نار	sheïwaṭ	شيوط	Fire.
ابيض	lebhem	لبهم	White.
احمر	ófir	اوفر	Red.
ماي كثير	Gí ríhó	كي ريهو	Plenty of Water.
ماي قليل	ríhó hararhen	ريهو حررهن	Scarcity of Water.
بير	eb-her	ابهر	A Well.
حبل	két	قيت	A Rope.
سكين	sári	صاري	A Knife.
قلم	ḳalam (Ar.)	قلم	A Pencil.
دوایه	dawáyah (Ar.)	دوایه	An Inkstand.
قرطاس	ḳarṭás (Ar.)	قرطاس	Paper.
اكتب	tó-kuttab (Ar.)	توكتب	To write.
كتاب	kitáb (Ar.)	كتاب	A Book.
جلد	jild (Ar.)	جلد	Skin or Hide.
كمه	kúfíyah (Ar.)	كوفيه	A Cap.
عمامه	'amámah (Ar.)	عمامه	A Turban.
ثوب	thób (Ar.)	ثوب	A Shirt.
حزام	arádí	ارادي	A Sash, or Girdle.
وزرا	makhfáf (Ar.)	مخفاف	Trowsers.
صندوق	ṣandúḳ (Ar.)	صندوق	A Box or Chest.
كرسي	kursí (Ar.)	كرسي	A Chair.
صحن	ṣaḥan (Ar.)	صحن	A Plate or Dish.
مهفه	merúhah (Ar.)	مروحه	A Fan.
مدفع	medfa' (Ar.)	مدفع	A Cannon.

ARABIC.		SOCOTRAN.	
باروت	bárút (Ar.)	باروت	Gunpowder.
أصبر	selúbah	سلوبه	Stop! Gently!
اعطي	ṭáfa'ah	طافعه	To give.
اقبض	telú	تلو	Take hold.
اخرج	sherákaḥ	شراكح	Go away.
ارجع	taktátaḥ	تكتاح	Come here.
ازهق	taḥríz	تحريز	Kill.
اكثير	kín	كين	Plenty of any thing.
امشي	ta'óh	تعوه	Make haste!
أصحب	'addah faḥraï	عده فحري	To be on good terms.
اعدل	tá ṣaḥḥ (Ar.)	تاصح	To behave properly.
انطف	shemátó	شماتو	To converse
اضبط	'arr	عرّ	Take hold.
اصعد	alleh	الح	To ascend.
انزل	ta-káfah	تقافه	To descend.
اجلس	istaḥall (Ar.)	استحل	Sit down.
اقرا	takárí (Ar.)	تقاري	To read.
اعمر	tanáfa' (Ar.)	تنافع	To mend.
اخرب	ta-nú'ash (Ar.)	تنوعش	To spoil.
افرش	ta-ásaf (Ar.)	تاصف	To spread any Mat or Bed.
احسب	ta ḥeïsib (Ar.)	تحيسب	To count.
اشرط	shálim	شالم	To stake a Bargain.
اضرب	tawajjah (Ar.)	توجه	To beat.
لاتضرب	'en tájah	عن تاجه	Do not strike.
اكسر	ta-kása' (Ar.)	تكاسع	To break.

ARABIC.		SOCOTRAN.	
لا تكر	en-taftaf (Ar.)	ان تفطف	Do not break.
لا تشرط	'en elfirád	عن انفراد	Make no agreement.
لا تعطي	en tendeff	عن تندف	Do not give.
ودا	araḥ	ارح	Remove or take away.
ودي	araḥ yinúk	ارح ينوق	To take any thing away.
لا تودي	alà tiyé'í	علي طيعي	Do not take away.
جيب	nikyán	نكيان	To bring.
لا تجيب	alankah	النكه	Do not bring.
زين	díyah	ديه	Good or well.
ما هو زين	diya'	ديع	No good. Bad.
اكل	astà	استا	To eat.
ما اكل	an itúk	ان اتوك	I have not eaten.
تقرب	tú taher	تو تهر	Come very close.
تبعد	tetú saher	تتو صهر	Go away to a distance.
آدمي	Ḥeïheï	حيمي	A Man.
حي	aldḥáma'	الظامع	Alive.
مات	sámí	صامي	Dead.
شمس	shohúm	شهوم	The Sun.
ظلال	míl'au	ميلعو	A Roof, or Top, Awning, &c.
تكلم	shemtar	شمتر	Dressed well, or in good clothes.
قريب	shíkah	شيكه	Close to.
بعيد	serhoḳ	سرحق	At a distance off.
ايش عندك	en mishaḳ	امهشق	What have you got?

ARABIC.		SOCOTRAN.	
صدق	āmak	آمك	True or Truth.
كذب	tubat	تبت	Untrue—a Falsehood.
اخذ	tez'en	تزعن	Take hold.
لا تاخذ	'en tez'en	عن تزعن	Do not take hold.
لا تجلس	takáta' (Ar.)	تقاطع	Do not sit down.
لا توقف	tatúhar	تطوهر	Do not stand.
ارقد	t'shúf	تشوق	To sleep.
اسبح	tebáh (té-sobáh ?)	تباح	To wash.
انظر	ta-ta'eïr	تتعير	To look.
لا تنظر	'en ta'eïr	عن تعير	Do not look.
انكر	teüber	تيبر	Broken.
تعال قريب	tekúde'n	تكودعن	Come near.
روح بعيد	tó'ad serhok	توعد سرحق	Go away.
اعطني ماي	abí ríhó	أبي ريهه	Bring some water.
ماي بحر	ríhó darnaham	ريهه درنهم	Salt water.
اشتري	astinjar	أستن جر	To buy.
بيع	kathú'am	كثوعم	To sell.
ابيع	eshímah	أشيمه	I will sell.

NOTATIONS

0 - When Sir Thomas Roe visited it be found horses.

1 - Stories of treasures hidden by the Portuguese are still fondly clung to by the natives, but I could never learn that, with the exception of the above fragments, any thing of importance was found.

2 - The practice which excludes females in all Muslim countries from assemblies' is rigidly adhered to by the Arabs of Socotra, and we did not therefore see the brides - though we were assured they were pretty.

3 - This must not be considered as an extortion, for they knew that our own Lascars might have been landed to take them up. I was, however, unwilling, as all were busy on board, to trouble our commander for them.

4 - A coarse woollen cloth, manufactured and used in Arabia.

5 - Camlet or camelot, a woollen-cloth, supposed to be made of camel's hair

6 - Holcus sorghum, or Sorghum vulgare. Sorgo is an Italian word; dhurrah, or dhorrah, being the Egyptian term.

7 - Probably in Ethiopic, which was commonly called Chaldean in the XVIth centur.-Vide Adelung's Mithridates, vol. i. p. 407. The people of Socotra were Christians at that time

8 - The resemblance between some of the above and the Arabic is very striking; but in looking over this as well as the vocabulary, the proximity of the island to the continents on either hand must not be forgotten, as it may have given rise to a variety of words and usages, common to them, though the people otherwise have ever remained distinct.

9 - Dhokn, or dokn; i. e. Sorghum sarcharatum-the Dab-d'hén of the Hindus

10 - Rhammus, or Zizyphus - Lotus, or Spina christi.

INDEX

Index
 A
  Abdallah (Chief of Hadibu), 3, 6, 14, 16, 26, 49-53, 68
  Abdullah (Sultan), 82
  Agriculture, xxii, 78,
  Al Muwaylih (Red Sea), xi
  Aloe sp (incl Socotrine Aloe *Aloe perryi*), 4, 5, 32, 39, 40, 54, 63, 71, 76, 77, 86
  Amaro (tree) 46
  Amaro (village), 55
  Animals *see* Fauna
  Ants, 60, 68, 81
  Arabs > 9, 13, 25, 31, 44, 63, 64, 68, Character, 7, 26, 32, 44, 49, 50-52, 54 > Customs, 21, 24, 28, 56, 71, 78, 83 > Dwellings, 13, 55 > Relations with Bedouins, 15, 18
  Assett tree, 57, 63, 77
  Atmosphere *see* Climate
 B
  Bahee Rahow (Tribe), 90
  Bats, 42, 82
  Beans, 67, 79
  Bedouins (Mountain people) > 24, 25, 26, 40, 46, 47, 48, 50, 57, 60, 76, 77, 78, 82, 83, 84, 88-92, 94 Appearance and Physique, 43, 56, 58> Caves and Dwellings, 31, 32, 41, 63, 85, 86 > Character and Manners, 7, 17, 22, 31, 42, 51, 55, 64, 66, 67, 71, 83, 87, 89> Diet & Food, 26, 28, 39, 58, 80 > Women, 28, 56, 67, 84

Birds, xix, 89
Bohain tree, 36, 57, 63, 68, 78
Boswellia (Frankincense), xviii, xix, xx, 5
Boxwood, Hildebrandt's (*Buxus hildebrandtii*), 16, 19, 20, 59, 73, 78, 87
British, viii, ix, xii, xiii, xiv,xvii, xxi, ,
Buteo socotraensis (Socotra Buzzard), xix

C

Cadhoop *see* Qadub
Camels (*Camelus dromedarius*) > hire of, 3, 7 > use and treatment, xii, 6, 8, 10-13, 16, 20, 22, 24-26, 31, 32, 33, 36, 39, 41, 44, 46, 47, 53, 57, 60, 64, 66, 67, 71, 77-79, 81, 82, 91, 93,
Camhane tree (*Dendrosicyos socotranus*), 13, 63, 77
Caves, xviii. xx, 13, 16, 22, 23, 24, 25, 27, 28, 29, 30, 31, 42, 46, 54, 59, 60, 63, 68, 86,
Centipedes, 58, 81
Christianity > Historical presence, xx, xxi, 11, 13, 31, 52, 66, 92-94
Civet Cat, 41, 42, 79, 81
Climate, 8, 21, 36, 37, 63, 75, 85, 86
Clothing, 47, 48, 50, 54, 56, 65, 71, 72, 85, 86, 91,
Coal (Depot), x, xiii, 5, 6, 17, 49
Collesseah *see* Qalansiyah
Coral, xviii, xix, 5, 7, 9, 19
Cotton plant, 60, 75
Cruttenden, Charles (Midshipman), xii, xiii, xvii, xxii, 10, 16, 26, 28, 51, 58, 68

D

Dancing, 21, 50, 87
Date Palms (*Phoenix dactylifera*), 1, 2 7, 8, 9, 13, 14, 19, 29, 32, 47, 53, 54, 55, 57, 59, 63, 67, 70, 71, 74, 78, 79, 86, 91, 94
Delisha, 69 (image)
Diseases / Fevers, xiii, xxi, , 60, 91

Djebel Haggier (Haggier Mountains), xviii, 48
Djebel Rummel, 2, 9
Dragon's Blood Tree (*Pterocarpus draco / Dracaena cinnabari*) > vii, 5, 32, 40, 47, 48, 55, 57, 61, 63, 68, 71, 76, 77, 86,
Dress *see* Clothing

E

East India Company (EIC), xxi,
Eshaib tree, 19, 22, 24, 36, 57, 69, 78
Eshall (Wadi/Valley), 57, 58, 66

F

Fadan Derafonte, 71

INDEX

Fadan Matallah, 24, 40
Farming *see* Agriculture
Fauna & Flora, 76-83
Feldspar, 46, 53, 54, 56, 58, 66, 67, 70,
Fishing, 14, 32, 90
Frankincense (*Boswellia*), xviii, xix, xx, 5

G

Geology, xviii, 12, 22, 41, 54, 73-75
Ghee, 8, 14, 24, 26, 32, 55, 79, 80, 82, 86, 87, 91
Goats, xxii, 8, 15, 20, 22, 23, 25, 27, 29, 31, 35, 39, 41, 42, 47, 59, 64, 66, 68, 79, 80, 86, 87, 89, 91
Government (Island), 82, 83
Granite Mountains, 2, 7, 45, 46, 54, 57, 63, 71, 74, 75, 78, 79, 90
Graves *see* Tombs

H

Hackabee, 59, 60
Hadibu (Tamarida) 1, 3, 5, 6, 7, 9, 11, 14, 15, 16, 26, 31, 39, 40, 41, 47, 49, 50, 53, 55, 58, 68, 71, 72, 74, 75, 76, 79-83, 90, 92, 94, 95
Haines, Captain Stafford B., xii, xviii
Hamed (Guide), 10, 11, 16, 26, 27, 40, 41
Hamed ben Tary (Chief), 49, 50, 82

I

Indigo, 75
Inscriptions, xx, 9, 13, 19, 20, 40
Insects, 81
Irrigation, 37

L

Lahsee (Tribe), 71
Language (Socotran) 3, 18, 28, 48, 64, 87, 88, > Vocabulary list, 96-105
Limestone, 12, 15, 23, 31, 39, 67, 74 90,
Locusts, xvi, 81

M

Maasah Sadan, 54
Mahrah (Tribe/Arabs), xii, xx, 63, 68, 92
Makkan Al Shiebah, 31, 40, 44
Marriage, 21, 87, 94
Medical, 38, 51, 66, 88
Millet, Pearl (*Pennisetum glaucum*), 8, 54, 55, 63, 66, 72, 75, 78, 79, 81, 86, 88
Monsoons, x, xviii, xx, 2, 5, 15, 24, 29, 32, 59, 60, 72, 74, 75, 76, 78, 91
Mosques, 32, 94
Mountains, xviii, 1, 6, 7, 8, 11, 13, 15-17, 22, 24-29, 32, 33, 39, 40, 42, 45, 46, 48, 57-59, 63, 64, 67, 70-76, 79, 80, 84-86, 90,

INDEX

Muscat, 9, 14, 50, 77, 79, 80, 88, 90

N

Natural History, 79-82
Natural Products, 76-79
Noged, 66, 71
Numbers (Socotran) 88

O

Oranges, 71, 79

P

Palinurus (Ship), x, xi, xii, xiii, xvi, 5, 10, 69
Phoenix dactylifera see Date Palms
Portuguese > 71, 72, 82, 88 Forts and Ruins, xxi, 5, 9, 15, 94, > History, xx, 9, > Influence on tribes, 39, 83, 90, 93,

Q

Qadi (Cadhi), 51, 52, 94
Qadub (Cadhoop/Kathoop), 13, 14, 15, 19, 25, 41, 49, 74, 82, 83, 90,
Qalansiyah (Collesseah), 6, 10, 11, 12, 13, 15, 17, 30, 31, 32, 34, 36, 39, 41, 50, 57, 67, 76, 79, 82, 83, 90, 94,
Qishn (Kisseen), xii, xx, 3, 6, 30, 50, 82, 87

R

Ramadan, xii, 38, 50, 92
Ras Feling, 67, 73
Ras Moree, 19, 20, 54, 58, 67, 70, 73, 74, 75, 79, 89, 90,
Religion, 40, 84, 87, 92, 93, 94,
Reservoirs (Water), 10, 24, 25, 37, 40, 44, 67, 68, 74

S

Sheep, xxii, 2, 8, 15, 16, 17, 18, 20, 21, 22, 23, 25-29, 31, 37, 38, 40-42, 47, 54-56, 58, 59, 63, 64, 66-68, 77-80, 86, 87, 90,
Shells, xviii, 19, 42
Skins (animal), xxii, 18, 19, 23, 29, 31, 34, 35, 76, 86,
Slaves, 10, 22, 25, 26, 50, 52, 60, 64, 83, 90, 91
Snakes & snake totem, 20, 81
Socotran Pomegranate (*Punica protopunica*), 22, 25, 78
Streams, 2, 8, 11, 13, 19, 20, 22-25, 32, 34, 41,42, 46, 47, 53-57, 60, 63, 64, 66, 67, 69, 70, 72-75, 79,
Suleiman (Guide), 10, 41, 44, 56, 90,
Sultan of Qishn, xii, xiii, xviii, xx, xxi, 3, 30, 49, 50, 82, 84
Sunday (Servant), xii, 47, 50-52, 60, 66
Suq (Suk), xx, 9, 72

T

Tamarind (*Tamarindus indica*), 45, 46, 70, 78
Tamarida *see* Hadibu

Tobacco, 2, 7, 8, 20, 21, 26, 48, 60, 79, 87
Tombs and Graves, xiii, 9, 78, 92, 95
Trees, 76-79 *see also specific species*
Trial by Ordeal, 89
Tribes, 83, 89
Tuk tree (Wild Fig), 36, 68, 69, 78

V

Vocabulary, 97-106
Vultures, 29, 82

W

Wahhabis, xxi, 7, 9, 88, 95
Weaving, 23, 86
Wellsted, James Raymond, viii-xviii
Whale/Whalers, xix, xxii, 2, 18
Witchcraft (gouls), 88
Women > 8, Arab, 50, > Bedouin, 26, 28, 39, 47, 56,

Z

Zanzibar, 7, 9, 14, 90
Ziziphus spina-christi (Nebek/Sidr), 17, 18, 21, 22, 24, 25, 31, 40, 57, 63, 69, 86, 88

THANK YOU 🙏 for buying this book.
I do hope you found it an interesting insight.
A review will help let others know if it's right for them.
It will also let us know what we need to improve.

PHOTOGRAPHS

Creative Commons License from Flickr
    All below have been edited for printing with historic names & functions used
    Aloe spicata Ton Rulkens
    Ras Qalansiyah Dan
    Ras Summare lagoon Qalansiyah Gerry & Bonni
    Cadoop Valerian Guillot
    Wdi Dirhur Gerry & Bonni
    Goat Skins for Water Rod Waddington
    Diksam Plateau, Haggier Mountains Dan
    Dragon blood trees (Dracaena cinnabari) at dawn on Firmhin Plateau, Valerian Guillot
    Dragon blood trees (Dracaena cinnabari) at dawn on Firmhin Plateau, Cover Valerian Guillot
    Dragons Blood (Dracaena cinnabari) Cover Hope Hill
    Dragons Blood (Dracaena cinnabari) & Camel Firmhin Plateau Valerian Guillot
    Adenium socotranum - Hope Hill
    Delisha Beach Valerian Guillot
    Di Hamri coral reefs Gerry & Bonni
    Frankincense (Boswellia sp) east of Hadiboh Valerian Guillot
    Date Palms and Dragons Blood Firman Haggier Mountains Rod
    Geez script Valerian Guillot
    from Wikipedia
    Civet (Civettictis civetta) amanderson2

PHOTOGRAPHS

Satellite Nasa

Socotra Maps James Wellsted

Meat cooked on Stones Arabesque
    Nebek (Ziziphus spina christi) Arabesque
    Egyptian Vulture (Neophron percnopterus) Arabesque
    Natural Tamerind (Tamarindus indica) Arabesque

www.ingramcontent.com/pod-product-compliance
Lightning Source LLC
Chambersburg PA
CBHW011317080526
44588CB00020B/2738